Building a Personal Culture to Win

Expanding Your Personal Frontier of Human Achievement

By Rob Ffield

Inspire On Purpose Publishing

Irving, Texas

Building a Personal Culture to Win
Expanding Your Personal Frontier of Human Achievement

Inspire On Purpose Publishing
Irving, Texas
(888) 403-2727

http://inspireonpurpose.com

The Platform Publisher™

Printed in the United States of America

Library of Congress Control Number: 2014953156

ISBN 13: 978-1-941782-03-3

TABLE OF CONTENTS

Dedication

To the Noble Calling in each of us, and to those who have the courage to go for it.

Introduction:
Go for It!

"Ice, your life just changed forever."

When my mentor, a former Blue Angel, uttered these words to me, I was sure he was talking about the excitement of the airshows, the incredible people I would meet, and the fact that my family and I would be moving to the white sandy beaches of Pensacola, Florida: "The Cradle of Naval Aviation."

It was spring of 2000 and I had just been selected to command and be the Flight Leader of the Navy Flight Demonstration Squadron, better known as the U.S. Navy Blue Angels.

I now realize that he was referring to something much bigger.

He was talking about the positive, personal transformation that happens to each of us when we decide to go for a goal that is seemingly out of our reach. And we win.

Building a Personal Culture to Win: Expanding Your Personal Frontier of Human Achievement is about setting the stage for reaching your life goals. This plan will help you not only reach those goals, but align your goals with your personal "Noble Calling" so that you will feel compelled to move forward, to relentlessly innovate, and to catapult to success beyond your wildest dreams.

In my case, my challenge was to rapidly learn the art and science of leading the Blue Angels in the most demanding, low-altitude, high-speed flying environments known to humanity. My teammates and I also had to uphold the Blue Angels' world-class reputation for precision and skill, while representing the men and women of our armed forces.

What we learned from that experience is that it does not matter if your goal is Earth-shattering in scope or a simple step forward. By adhering to the same principles outlined here in what I am calling the *CATSHOT 13*™ program, anyone can overcome a real or perceived lack of skill, a shortage of resources, or even a subconscious fear of failure.

Within these pages are three key lessons we learned: Every goal worth pursuing in this world has challenges. You will never have all of the time, resources, or skills that you would like. Once you reach your goal, you will always find more ways to improve yourself and push your boundaries even further.

My years of experience with the Blue Angels, as well as two tours with another top military aviation organization—the U.S. Navy Fighter Weapons School, better known as TOPGUN—taught me that world-class organizations attract world-class people. They face the same issues that anyone does in the workplace, but with much higher stakes. Errors at that level can lead to serious injury or even death.

I learned that the top players on the top teams possessed three overarching characteristics that led to their success—*Passion, Free Will,* and *Focus*—what I call the *Performance Triad*™, a concept we will explore further in these pages.

This *Performance Triad,* when paired with your *Noble Calling,* will help you overcome any real or perceived roadblocks, disregard unproductive comments from well-meaning friends and family, and perform your best with thoughtful, consistent assessments of your progress as you move toward your goal.

The following chapters will show you how to recognize and overcome obstacles so that you can experience a powerful transformation that will expand your personal frontier of human achievement.

My Personal *CATSHOT 13* Process

My *CATSHOT 13* process is based on my extensive experience as a two-time combat instructor pilot at TOPGUN, as well as a Commanding Officer and Flight

Leader for the Blue Angels. I have also used many of these techniques on the ground, leading the staffs of three-star and four-star generals, and through my current management consulting business.

I developed and honed this 13-week program after years of teaching people to accomplish extreme goals in extreme environments. If the process works under those conditions, it certainly will work for you.

If you have never heard of a CATSHOT, it is the term that Naval Aviators use for a catapult shot. It refers to the moment that a jet is launched by catapult off of a ship at sea; it is perhaps the most intense experience in aviation.

Here is how I described it in my first book, *Building a Culture to Win: Expanding the Frontier of Human Achievement.*

> "The CATSHOT — which takes only seconds — represents the transition point from the planning and preparation phase of a mission to the actual mission execution phase. It is here that we see the culmination of all of our plans put into motion. It is here that we see our momentum in play. It is here that we see the direction our plans are heading.
>
> In flight, as [with any goal], you must begin with thorough and methodical pre-mission planning. Everything related to the goals of your mission must be planned, briefed,

and reviewed. Before you can initiate your CATSHOT, you must make sure you have a precise alignment of all your crewmembers, and of all the key technical systems.

Once the CATSHOT is made, your aircraft—or goal—is in motion, and the execution of your plan begins. The execution of your plan is the most exciting part of the process. However, we will learn in this book that the importance of having a plan to land and a plan to debrief are key to your continued success.

If you want to continue to improve and have lifelong success, each mission—or project— must be assessed for both its successes and its failures. Capturing lessons learned helps you to adjust goals and tactics in real time, allowing you to improve the execution of future missions and improve your bottom line."

If you want your life to change forever, like mine did when I joined the Blue Angels, you must develop an infinite loop from execution to lessons to improvement to execution, and around again. I will help you develop the tools to create such a process, based on the lessons that I learned flying the skies with the Blue Angels and TOPGUN.

Building a Culture to Win: Expanding the Frontier of Human Achievement focused on how to build world-class teams, using the lessons I learned during my time with the Blue Angels and TOPGUN organizations.

This book focuses those same lessons on *you* — the individual. You will learn practical steps and methods to improve your personal performance and tackle any goal you set. What you learn here will help you achieve personal goals, as well as work well in a team.

These pages, and those of the companion guide — the *CATSHOT 13* **Personal Operations Handbook (POH)** — will help you learn to follow your gut, to hone your instincts, and to then methodically improve your skills in order to expand your frontier of achievement and success.

When you identify your goals and make the decision to accept the challenge, this book will not only help you, it will change your life forever.

No matter how young or old you are, and no matter how big, small, or well-defined your goals, when you read *Building a Personal Culture to Win: Expanding Your Personal Frontier of Human Achievement*, you will gain a simple understanding of what drives your success. And this understanding will propel you toward your goal.

This book is about going beyond theory and taking action.

Most importantly, when you merge these *CATSHOT 13* principles with the self-developed guide in your *CATSHOT 13* POH, you will quickly experience progress.

Some of you may have a well-defined goal in life already.

Others may not. In either case, this book will help you more clearly define your goals in a way that will allow your daily choices to lead to a joyful, fulfilled, wealthy, and purposeful life.

Will you accept the challenge to go for it?

If the status quo is good enough for you, you need read no further. But if you want to change your life, keep reading.

For those of you truly eager to get started, I am confident that you can devour this book over a long, leisurely weekend. Only after you plow through the text will you be prepared to jump on the 13-week, self-coached course found in the *CATSHOT 13* POH.

During this 13-week process, you will discover how to fine-tune your personal **Performance Triad**. After you read this book and gain a better understanding of the concepts, I recommend you go to the CATSHOT website (http://catshotgroup.com/productsservices/books) and download our easy-to-follow handbook. This will save you time as you work through the program. This same *CATSHOT 13* POH also functions as your personal logbook, or journal, which you can customize to meet your specific needs. It is designed to help you track your progress by recording various metrics in the areas of health and personal and professional skills throughout a 13-week period. If you do not have access to a printer, or you prefer to create your own logbook, you may simply review the POH format available online to use as a model.

This book prepares you for successfully following the *CATSHOT 13* process. Each chapter introduces the key concepts you will use to dial in on your personal Performance Triad, and reinforces these concepts by including short exercises designed to stimulate your thoughts.

These techniques are proven to help you perform at your highest level, whether working alone or with a team. They will help you develop and sustain motivation by showing progress and providing interim wins along the way, something many programs fail to do.

In addition, *CATSHOT 13* is a reusable program. Once you complete one 13-week cycle, you are encouraged to start over and improve your results even further. A key component of the *CATSHOT 13* program is that we learn to continually strive for improvement, or relentlessly innovate.

The size of the goal does not matter. But if the goal requires you to step outside of your comfort zone, requires skills or resources that you may not currently have, or requires you to overcome the fear of failure, *CATSHOT 13* can help you.

For those who have extreme goals, this process will help you safely achieve them by building your capacity to achieve with a building-block approach. If this process can take a fleet jet pilot and transform him/her into a Blue Angel in just three months, imagine what it can do for you.

Turn the page to begin your personal CATSHOT!

Section 1:

"Let's Run 'Em Up"

Get Fired Up and Ready for Your
Catapult Shot to Success

T he sun was just beginning to peek through the early morning, low-hanging clouds that hovered precariously above me as I sat on the flight deck of the USS George Washington (CVN-73) in my fully loaded Boeing F/A-18 Hornet fighter jet.

The 37,000 pounds of steel that surrounded me was connected by a steam catapult line to the aircraft carrier in the middle of the ocean. In a few minutes, my F/A-18 and I would be shot down the catapult track at such a high rate of speed that we would clear the 1,000-plus-feet deck in a matter of seconds.

This is the catapult shot, or CATSHOT. It is when the planning ends and the execution begins. It is the exact moment you launch your ideas and see them transformed into reality.

The energy I felt about to be unleashed was incredible. Thousands of pounds of thrust from my jet engines and extreme pressure from the steam below would soon take me from standing still to being instantly airborne and accelerating upward at an eye-watering rate.

To prepare for this moment, I planned every aspect of my mission. Whether it was my very first catapult shot or my one-thousandth, I knew I had to have total alignment of mission and goal, a mental and physical preparedness, and complete awareness of the environment around me.

But I am not doing this alone. I have a team, a team that must understand my mission and my goal as clearly as I do. Otherwise, they cannot properly support me.

As I am given the signal to run up my engines to full power, I go over my takeoff checklist one more time: brakes off, flight control, trim, set.

The catapult officer looks directly at me, waiting for me to signal that I am ready.

I give him a crisp, clear hand salute and put my head back on my headrest in preparation for the shot of acceleration. Then, I wait to be transformed.

* * *

As with a CATSHOT, all great human achievement occurs when there is a similar alignment of goals, mission, and readiness. To create this alignment, you must identify your *Noble Calling* and balance your personal *Performance Triad* of *Passion, Free Will,* and *Focus.*

Passion is what makes you live, eat, and breathe your personal and professional goals, thus creating momentum. It is the fuel that drives individuals to achieve at the highest levels.

Free Will is the oxygen that makes the fires of passion burn hotter. It must be properly harnessed to fuel innovation and drive continuous improvement and relentless innovation.

Focus is what hones the momentum created by your passion and directs your free will to accomplish more than you thought possible. It is the heat that takes you to the next level of performance.

Performance Triad: The three elements of the Performance Triad — Passion, Free Will, and Focus — must be balanced in order for us to function at our optimal level. Just as a fire must be continually managed to produce a flame, you should continually adjust these three elements to produce your best results.

Noble Calling: Your Noble Calling is your ultimate purpose in life. It is the "true north" for all of your life goals, both personal and professional. This is what drives you to perform, to overcome obstacles, and to sacrifice instant gratification for long-term success.

In Section 1, you will prepare to begin your own CATSHOT by:

- Identifying your inspired *Noble Calling* and your *Passion*

- Developing a plan for relentless innovation and harnessing your *Free Will*

- Cultivating an unwavering persistence and concentration, or *Focus*

- Maximizing achievement by aligning these three pillars to create your personal *Performance Triad*

Let's begin!

Chapter 1:

Your Inspired Noble Calling—Passion

"Easing the pull," I say in a calm cadence to the five Blue Angel wingmen. They must be able to easily synchronize their movements with mine or we will all be dangerously out of position.

"Rolling out the Delta Right Pitch Up Break."

We are flying a mere 150 feet above the show line, at 400 miles per hour, just inches apart in our Delta Formation. We look like a flock of high-powered, gleaming metal geese with me in the lead.

"Boss is breaking," I say just as I give my jet a snap up to clear the formation with 7Gs of force. I quickly roll 90 degrees to my right and pull another 7Gs in a sustained right, 180-degree turn in preparation for landing.

This is the last aerial maneuver of our standard 45-minute air demonstration sequence. This scenario could have been any one of the hundreds of air shows I led as the Flight Leader of the US Navy Flight Demonstration Squadron, better known as the Blue Angels.

Performing flight demonstrations in front of millions of spectators a year, showcasing the pride and professionalism of the US Navy and Marine Corps was my dream job. How did I get here? What led me to this line of "work"? Let me tell you.

In reality, I never considered performing with the Blue Angels a "job." In fact, I have never considered any job in my chosen profession to be "work."

Aviation was my lifelong passion.

After seeing a Naval Aviation recruiting poster, I quit my job as a well-paid aerospace engineer for the remote chance to fly fighters with the Navy. A move many told me was foolish.

"Why give up a great paying job as an engineer, especially when there is no guarantee from the Navy that they will even make you a pilot?" my family and friends would ask me.

Despite the odds, I took the leap and I never looked back. When I entered the Navy to pursue aviation, I knew I had found my true calling. The passion I had for learning and applying myself in this field was at a level I had never felt before. That passion led me to a string of successes in a career that lasted well over 20 years—from being one of the first to fly the newest fighters at the time, the F/A-18 Hornet, to two tours as a TOPGUN instructor, command (CEO) at the squadron and air wing levels, to leading the Blue Angels.

Not one day seemed like work. This was what I was meant to do.

What made it even better was that I saw my career as a Noble Calling. I was helping to protect Americans and our country. Nothing was going to stop me from being the best.

Passion: The Fuel

Passion is the fuel that drives you to achieve. When you find your passion, you will see how easy it is to exceed your own expectations, and possibly even exceed the accomplishments of almost everyone else in your chosen field.

Few people take the time to identify their passion, let alone take the risks necessary to pursue it. Therefore, by taking the steps outlined in this book to help you identify your passion, you will find yourself part of an elite group.

My switch from aviation engineering to flying fighter jets was my first experience in finding and following my passion. Finding my passion truly was the fuel that gave me the energy to devote 27 years of my life to working long hours in demanding environments. And I considered it a privilege to do so.

Passion is the fuel that propels you to work every day. When you can pair this with your Noble Calling, you can catapult your motion to achieve faster and higher goals.

Noble Calling: Your Steam Catapult

Taking your passion to the next level—identifying how it relates to your Noble Calling—will make you the envy of all of those around you. Have you ever noticed how people gravitate toward world-class people and teams? It is because they want to find the same level of success and experience the same feeling of satisfaction.

Don't worry, at this point, if you do not know what your Noble Calling is. You may not even know what ignites your passion yet. That's okay.

It took me several years before I could identify my passion. Remember, I started out as an engineer. I was well down the path of what looked like success in that field when I discovered that I needed to change course if I was going to follow my Noble Calling with passion.

At first, my passion was primarily about the excitement of flying, the thrill of being a fighter pilot. As I gained experience, my vision became clearer. I began to view my chosen profession as more than a career that ignited my passion. I saw it as a true Noble Calling.

My military aviation career gave me a strong feeling of patriotism. I was proud to uphold the traditions of those before me who had fought to keep this country free. This concept of a Noble Calling strengthened my passion for service to others as I gained seniority.

Your Noble Calling will likely be something bigger than yourself. For example, because my Noble Calling was to serve my country, I developed a strong desire to make sure that the next generation could continue what I had inherited from those before me. I felt it was my duty to pass on my experience and commitment to those who would carry the torch of excellence forward.

In addition, a Noble Calling can propel you to greater accomplishments by fueling your passion. I found that as I reached more and more career milestones, my aspirations began to expand further and further. Every time I reached a goal, I would revisit and revise my life plan. I was amazed at what I ultimately was able to achieve.

While my passion for aviation was a strong motivator, it was not until I discovered my Noble Calling that I realized aviation was just one of many passions that could help me realize this Noble Calling. Therefore, when the day came that I could no longer fly, I still had direction—I wanted to continue to be a part of making America strong.

Today, I use the lessons I learned during my military aviation career to teach the next level of leaders who can make America strong. I have determined that no matter what job I have, I will always give back to my country. My passion for aviation is just one way for me to do just that. My passion for excellence is another way, and my passion for leadership is yet another.

That focus on my Noble Calling has brought all of my experiences and passions together to inspire and assist others to reach their goals. It is what led me to identify the Performance Triad and to develop the *CATSHOT 13* POH. I am confident that these tools will help you achieve success in whatever field you choose.

I believe this concept of a Noble Calling is why many famous and wealthy Americans look for ways to give back. Carnegie, Rockefeller, Gates, and Oprah are some of the most famous, but there are many others.

It is also why parents and grandparents often find the most rewarding periods of their lives to be when they pass their knowledge and experiences on to their children and grandchildren.

It is why volunteerism is so rewarding to so many. Look at the top sports stars. Almost everyone is involved in a special community project, because it just feels right.

A Noble Calling goes beyond the superficial—it truly is a calling of a higher level.

You may be just starting out and have a ways to go before you will have the resources to make your big dent in the world. It doesn't matter. This book will still help you find your passion and attach it to your Noble Calling, so you can begin to make your mark in the world now.

What Is Your Noble Calling?

Identifying your Noble Calling is essential for you to reach your full potential. You may be very successful when following your passion. However, when you pair that passion with a Noble Calling, the sky is not even the limit!

This importance of a Noble Calling is particularly evident at life's many transition points—whether you are starting your first job, moving up the corporate ladder, transitioning to a new career, or starting your own business. It can even help in your personal life—whether you are considering marriage or making decisions on raising your children. How you make these decisions and carry them out will be easier and bring more success if you reflect on your Noble Calling in relation to each choice.

All of us go through these transition periods at some point in our lives. Those who know what their Noble Calling is and how to unleash their passion in that direction will weather these points well.

Sports stars, doctors, teachers, parents, and students— everyone gets to a point when their current professional or personal situation is no longer viable. Professionals must retire, students must graduate, and mothers and fathers must change their focus when their children move out of the house.

Even fighter pilots eventually have to stop flying fighter jets.

Many people flounder at these points in their lives. Without the direction of a Noble Calling and an understanding of our passion, we can find ourselves unable to move forward. We might even take opportunities that do not suit us because they are convenient or because someone else suggested them. Or because we just don't know what else to do.

The *CATSHOT 13* POH will help you move forward by providing a method for you to outline your goals — long-term, mid-term, and short-term. Putting these goals in writing will allow you to begin to visualize and understand what you were meant to do.

Note that your long-term goals — your vision for your life — should drive your mid-term and short-term goals. In practice, most people look at short-term goals as tasks that they can easily accomplish and check off their list. They may have a vague connection to the person's purpose for their life or their career, but not always.

CATSHOT 13 is set up to help you maintain focus on all three levels of your goals — long-, mid-, and short-term — and their interconnectedness with a planning method that I call "Effects-Based Life Planning™." This method helps you set goals that are precise and clear, and assists you in visualizing yourself attaining these goals.

Effects-Based Life Planning

If you already know what your burning desire is—your passion in life or in your career—congratulations! That's a great position to be in, but this process can help you further refine your goals. It will challenge you to think in even larger terms and help you determine what you need to do to get there.

If you do not already have a clear plan, this process will help you find it. Even if your passion does not come to you right away, this process will help you prepare to achieve it when the sparks begin to fly.

The basic premise of Effects-Based Life Planning is to begin with the end in mind. In other words, imagine yourself at 100 years of age. You are having a big celebration and your loved ones have gathered to celebrate your life.

What are they saying about you? How are they describing your life? Your accomplishments? Your contributions to your family, your community, the world at large?

What effect do you want to have made on the world around you?

Once you have visualized the impact you would like your life to have, you can begin to identify the actions that will create those effects. You can also look for patterns and common elements among the various aspects of your life to more clearly pinpoint what you are passionate about, and to define your Noble Calling.

Clarity of Vision

CATSHOT 13 will help you dig deeper and create a clearer vision of where you are going and what your life will look like when you get there. It will help you zero in on your passion and your Noble Calling.

My passion for aviation and my Noble Calling to protect my country led me to volunteer for every exciting flying job I could. Human Resources professionals in the Navy made valiant attempts to redirect my energies to a more conventional path that would lead me up the ranks toward Admiral.

Had I listened to these well-meaning naval officers, I would have left the flight lines to take staff jobs earlier in my career. Staff jobs are fine for those with that passion, that Noble Calling. However, my passion was flying.

By following my passion, I earned not one, but two tours as a TOPGUN instructor. My passion also took me on tours as a Flight Leader and a Commanding Officer of the Blue Angels.

In each case, I was told by almost everyone that pursuing too many exciting flying jobs would hinder my opportunity for promotion. In each case they were wrong. I was promoted early to the next rank several times. Why? Because anyone with my passion could not help but succeed.

One of the primary reasons people are not in touch with their Noble Calling is because they have lost their free will—their ability to think for themselves. This freedom to tap into their own gifts has either been taken from them or they have given it up voluntarily. In the next chapter, we will discuss the importance of free will and how we can find it and keep it.

Points to Remember

- *Passion* is the first element of the Performance Triad—the Fuel.

- Your *Noble Calling* is the most powerful kind of goal because it harnesses your emotional and spiritual energy to take you to the next level of achievement in life.

- The *CATSHOT 13* program will help you with the short-term goals or steps that will lead you to your bigger, long-term goals, keeping your Noble Calling in mind.

- *Effects-Based Life Planning* is the process through which you will identify, define, and refine your goals from your long-term Noble Calling to your short-term *CATSHOT 13* goals.

POH Exercise*

My Noble Calling: The effect I want to have on this world is . . . _____

_____

_____

I will achieve my Noble Calling by pursuing my passion to . . . _____

_____

_____

*Your *CATSHOT 13* Personal Operations Handbook is your personal logbook, or journal. It is designed to help you track your progress by recording various metrics in the areas of health and personal and professional skills throughout a 13-week period. You may create your own logbook or use the official *CATSHOT 13* Personal Operations Handbook, by downloading it at http://catshotgroup.com/productsservices/books.

At the end of each chapter, we have provided some exercises, like these, that are related to the *CATSHOT 13* POH. We recommend you look at the POH exercises in this book as an introduction to the process that the actual *CATSHOT 13* POH will walk you through. However, we also recommend you completely read through this book before you begin using the POH.

Chapter 2:

Liberating Your Human Spirit — Free Will

S an Diego is gorgeous in June.

When I arrived in 1988 for my first tour of duty with the U.S. Navy Fighter Weapons School, better known as TOPGUN, I was joining a world-class organization with a 20-year-old reputation for excellence. Its fighter pilot training program was second to none.

I was excited to be there and eager to take my place on this elite team.

Soon after I began, it became clear that this training program, while the best in the world, was not the best it could be. The training program was based on the immediate tactical needs of the Vietnam War for which it was originally developed. At that time, selected pilots from each fighter squadron were sent to Naval Air Station Miramar to quickly learn the latest tactics and procedures from the highly experienced cadre of TOPGUN instructors so that they could return directly to their squadrons and pass along what they had learned to those fighting in combat. Time was of the essence.

By the late 1980s, the proliferation of weapons systems was increasing every day, as was their lethality. In addition, the airplanes were becoming more and more complex. It was important to not only teach pilots how to use their weapons with precision, but also to train them on all of the other weapons systems they would face, as well as the tactics they would need to use. Plus, they needed to learn more sophisticated, methodical ways to train their own squadrons when they returned to the fleet.

My fellow TOPGUN instructors and I were given the goal of updating the program to deal with today's real-world scenarios. We were allowed to use our own free will, or choices and decisions, to rework the training program.

Our new program was bold and different from any other. We combined the best strategies and tactics from all other aviation-training programs, and created innovative ways to challenge our pilots for the new realities of combat.

With each iteration of the new training program, the team of TOPGUN instructors and I would relentlessly innovate.

We made significant changes to how TOPGUN was manned and equipped and how students, upon graduation, would be used as instructors in the fleet. We knew that with each round of innovation we were improving our pilot training.

These changes required shifting millions-of-dollars-worth of assets, changing the way students were taught, and reassessing how trained pilots were later assigned their duties. Such overarching changes met with equally strong resistance. Our team of passionate, relentless innovators continued to use their free will to navigate the political waters to figure out ways to make the new training program a reality.

The Power of Free Will

You do not have to be a fighter pilot to tackle the challenges that lie before you. Yet, you can learn some key lessons from this example about the importance of using your free will to make decisions on the job. If you relinquish your free will, you will be reduced to merely completing assigned tasks.

However, if you are passionate about your job and have found your Noble Calling, then you will want to liberate your own human spirit and exercise your free will to expand your frontier of human achievement beyond merely completing the task assigned to you.

By doing so, your career path will be yours. You will never "go to work" but, instead, will follow your passion. You will have a sense of authority and control over your job and your life, which alone is liberating and will elevate your spirit. It is like the oxygen you breathe. You need to add it to your Noble Calling to be successful.

Free will may seem to some to be counterintuitive as a teamwork skill. Yet, when properly harnessed, it serves as the oxygen for the fire fueled by passion. Free will stokes the fires of innovation and fuels continuous improvement. Managers who do not allow their staff to exercise free will are limiting their team's success.

Our *CATSHOT 13* process encourages you to be innovative with the tasks you must do every day to live. You can always find ways to be more efficient and to be better at just about anything. Striving for perfection, even if you never achieve it, is a healthy mindset. It is the mindset of a winner!

Be a Dreamer and a Relentless Innovator

As you embrace *CATSHOT 13*, you will learn to visualize success, to remind yourself to liberate your human spirit, and to use your free will to dream and relentlessly innovate until you reach your goals.

Relentless innovators are those people who continually strengthen and reinvent themselves and their goals. They see "no" as a challenge to be navigated, not a roadblock to be avoided.

Anyone who dares to push themselves to the next level of achievement will find that roadblocks are everywhere. It is not a matter of *if* but a matter of *when* you will reach one. Therefore, you must plan for the unexpected and embrace the challenges set before you.

This is where you would use your imagination to come up with new ideas for tackling old problems, whether it is synthesized imagination or creative imagination.

Synthesized imagination is when you take existing thoughts and ideas and combine them into something new. For example, inventor Johannes Gutenberg is believed to have created the printing press by merging the technologies of the wine press and the coin punch. This is the more common way ideas are developed.

Creative imagination is where you come up with a purely new idea that no one else has ever thought of before. Even many of these ideas are based on something existing, but they take it in a whole new direction. For example, the Wright Brothers studied birds to see how they fly, from that, they invented the airplane. They created a wing warping method for directional control to emulate the birds. Glen Curtis developed the aileron to circumvent the Wright Brothers wing-warping patent to achieve the same effect.

The *CATSHOT 13* program will help you identify your goals and their roadblocks, as well as help you develop your imaginations and the skills necessary to continually improve, or relentlessly innovate, those goals as you progress. Just as you would alter your exercise program when it becomes too easy by adding weights or reps, so will our program show you how to up the ante on your personal and professional goals as you begin to achieve them.

See It to Believe It: The Power of Visualization

Take a moment now to visualize achieving a small goal in the future that will lead to achieving a larger goal. Consider how you can achieve this goal while staying true to your passion and to your Noble Calling.

Now think of a time in the past when you achieved something significant. Take yourself back to that time and relive that aura of excitement you felt. Perhaps you were riding a bike, driving a car for the first time, negotiating a winning business deal, or a reaching a milestone in sports.

Where were you when it happened? What were you wearing? Who was with you? What were the sounds and smells around you? Close your eyes, drink it in, and remember all of the details.

Visualization is a tool long used by elite athletes, top military professionals, and world-class business leaders. You may have heard the line, "Be one with the ball." Some people say it as a joke, while many top athletes seriously visualize where the ball will go and how it will get there.

Most people have a vague notion of what they want: more money, a bigger house, early retirement, or the opportunity to be closer to family. However, you will never achieve your goal if you do not know *exactly* what it is, where it is, and how you generally plan to get there.

How much money? Do you need a few hundred dollars this month to pay your rent, or do you need $1 million so that you can retire early? The options, strategy, and planning for these two goals of "more money" are completely different. One may mean mowing a few lawns in the summer, while the other may require a long-term investment strategy.

Once you have more specifically defined your goal, close your eyes and visualize what it would feel like to achieve it. Think of the various ways you can achieve that goal and still follow your passion. Do not listen to what others would do. What would *you* do that is true to your own personal Noble Calling?

As you begin to achieve the smaller goals leading to your larger goals, that same excitement will be the oxygen, or the free will, that will be added to the fuel of your passion. This combination will help make your dreams come true.

There is one more essential element—in addition to passion and free will—that you will need, however, if you are going to CATSHOT yourself to success and wealth. It is focus.

As important as it is to use your free will to accomplish your goals, unbounded free will itself will not produce a winning outcome. The third leg of the Performance Triad is key to balancing the first two legs. We will learn more about this final leg in Chapter 3.

Points to Remember

- *Free Will* is the second element of the Performance Triad—the Oxygen.

- When you are allowed to exercise your free will in conjunction with your passion, you will naturally become a **Relentless Innovator**, someone who is always looking for a better way to accomplish the task at hand.

- It is important that individuals create and preserve an atmosphere that allows them to use their free will.

- It is critical that you take responsibility for your own actions. Carefully maintaining your health, fitness, financial situation, and personal relationships allows you to maintain your free will. Financial instability, personal upheaval at home, and poor health or fitness can dramatically diminish or completely strip away your free will.

- The *CATSHOT 13* program offers visualization exercises that will help you feel the excitement of reaching a goal, thus giving you more confidence that you can achieve that goal.

POH Exercise

How will you maximize your ability to use your free will in following your passion?

Free Will Statement

I will use my free will every day to follow my passion by:

a. Thinking critically for myself and selectively using the best suggestions from the following people/resources in the pursuit of my Noble Calling and my passion.

- _____
  _____
- _____
  _____
- _____
  _____

b. Always having the following positive counter tactics to any negative suggestions and influences, even though they may come from very close, well-meaning friends and family:

- _____
  _____
- _____
  _____
- _____
  _____

c. Striving to attain financial freedom by doing the following:

- _____
  _____

- _____

_____

- _____

_____

d. Taking the following positive steps to get myself out of a dependency situation, such as from the government, friends, family, parents:

- _____

_____

- _____

_____

- _____

_____

e. Overcoming my top three fears in life by:

- _____

_____

- _____

_____

- _____

_____

f. Dedicating time to discovery and innovation in my pursuit by:

- _____

_____

- _____

_____

- _____

_____

(Note: We recommend you use the complete, detailed version of this exercise from the POH, which can be found on http://catshotgroup. com/productsservices/books, after you have completely read through this book.)

Chapter 3:

Your Unwavering Persistence and Concentration—Focus

Jet Camp

Flying the precision formations of the Blue Angels requires extreme focus.

A passion for flying and the ability to use free will to make the necessary, split-second decisions required to stay in formation no matter the weather, wind, or mechanical conditions is crucial to our success, but they are not enough.

Focus is key.

Jet Camp, as many of us call it, is the time of year when the newbie Blue Angels—all of whom have years of top-notch flight experience and near-perfect records—are taught the maneuvers unique to this elite squadron.

The term *Jet Camp* may sound like a vacation, but it is far from it.

This group's Noble Calling was to represent the men and women of the U.S. Navy and Marine Corps who had been, or still were, serving in defense of our country.

Even though we were all experienced naval aviators and jet pilots, flying an airshow in Blue Angel fashion would be new to half of us every year (the team swaps out roughly half the pilots every 12 months).

During winter training, we would fly in tighter formations, closer to the ground, executing more precise aerobatic maneuvers than we ever did in our individual fleet squadrons. It is dangerous. It is exhilarating. It is hard to make it look easy.

Repetition was an integral part of our training. We would fly a maneuver over and over and over, until everyone — from the pilots to the ground crew — had their task down pat.

We started with the basics: A daily routine of mental preparation, rehearsal, briefing, debriefing, and flying three times a day. We began in mid-November and built our skills and camaraderie quickly. At the end of the three-month period of a focused, concentrated effort, we had developed a culture of excellence with muscle memory so ingrained that we were ready to perform in front of millions of spectators in a safe, yet extreme manner, anywhere in the world.

In addition to our physical readiness and mental alertness, we had to stave away colds and other ailments, even as we shook hands with thousands of people. It may seem like a trivial matter, but we could not afford to be sick even one day during the 300 days a year we would be on the road performing.

We had to do all of this while also presenting a positive image to the public—whether on "official" time or on our own "personal" time. Along the way, we each experienced personal and team successes and challenges. Through all the peaks, plateaus, and valleys in our performances, we focused on maintaining a positive attitude at all times.

This same building-block approach is used throughout the military, especially with some of the other extreme programs, such as TOPGUN and Navy SEALs. This book will give you the tools to create your own building-block approach when you develop your personalized *CATSHOT 13* program.

These concentrated training efforts, similar in many ways to how elite athletic teams prepare, have proven to be extremely effective in expanding human performance and achievement in a short period of time.

How? With focus.

Focus brings the heat to the fire. It is what hones the momentum created by your passion. It also harnesses your free will so that you can control your energy and direct it toward your goals.

The Fire Triangle

Fuel, oxygen, and heat are necessary to ignite a fire. Likewise, you need passion, free will, and focus — the Performance Triad — to produce world-class results. Let any leg of the triad fall away, and your results will suffer.

Passion and free will can bring you some success by making you stand out among your colleagues who are not as empowered. However, you will never accomplish world-class achievements or experience your own personal elite performance without also having focus.

Think of a piece of paper out in the sunshine. The sun provides heat. Oxygen is in the air. The piece of paper provides the fuel. However, paper sitting in the sun does not burst into flames on its own.

But if you take a magnifying glass and focus the sun's rays on the paper, you will soon have a fire.

The same is true for your efforts in achieving your Noble Calling. You have to focus your passion and your free will in a persistent, concentrated fashion before performance and achievement can help you reach your lofty goal.

CATSHOT 13 will help you organize your efforts around your Noble Calling, uniting your passion, free will, and focus in a building-block approach. This will help you focus your efforts in a persistent fashion so that you make steady progress toward achieving your goals.

Over time, the skills that you learn will form muscle and brain memory, which will create habits that will make winning and achieving results an integral part of your lifestyle and personal culture.

Focus on a Personal Culture to Win: Creating Winning Habits

CATSHOT 13 uses the same elements that many of the world's successful entrepreneurs, scientists, athletes, and business or political leaders have used to achieve great accomplishments. It concentrates these elements in an easy-to-follow program that works in real-world situations where time and resources are often limited.

As you learn, practice, and cultivate the key concepts of the Performance Triad discussed in these pages, we will help you begin to create winning habits that will take you further than you ever thought possible. These habits of constant improvement, relentless innovation, and focusing every action on the long-term goals that are aligned to your Noble Calling will serve you well in all aspects of your life.

When I flew F/A-18 fighter jets off of the deck of an aircraft carrier, I was the only guy in the cockpit, but I was never alone. The crew on the ground made sure that my multi-million-dollar fighter jet and I did not plummet into the sea. This ground crew was often made up of men and women barely out of high school. In the civilian world, they would be in entry-level jobs with little responsibility. Yet, on our aircraft carriers, they were literally the people who kept me alive to fly another day.

If we can teach these young people the skills and the work habits necessary for success, we can teach you too. Here are the key habits you must develop if you want to have a personal winning culture:

> ➤ Embrace your free will. You must feel free to express your entrepreneurial spirit in all that you do. This includes reaching out and doing great things within the bounds of your job or task. All organizations have rules in order to keep large groups of people and resources on task. However, if you want to excel, you will never follow orders without questioning them, and without, respectfully, offering more effective and efficient ways of doing things.

> ➤ Know your limits and when to adjust them. Rules are usually good to live by; they provide necessary structure. Over time, you will establish a set of rules for yourself that will lead to success. However, you should regularly review any and all rules you do set for yourself to ensure that they are still effective for the task at hand. Rules and processes should not be changed randomly, but through a conscious decision-making process that reveals a need to change due to revised realities.

➤ <u>Look out for team members.</u> If you are following your passion and working to achieve your Noble Calling, then you will likely attract others with similar goals and passions. Whether they are clients, customers, or coworkers, you should be excited to be working with them and, thus, take them into consideration when making decisions.

➤ <u>Watch out for so-called "experts."</u> When you need help accomplishing your goals, reach out to experts who can take you to the next level. However, make sure you understand exactly what they are doing for you, how they are doing it, and that they are continually performing with excellence. Do not hire outside experts and then relinquish control to them.

➤ <u>Clean jets fly better.</u> This is a saying that held true for my entire military flying career. It also applies in other areas of business and sports, such as auto racing. The best performers always look squared away. Likewise, your personal organization and cleanliness helps clear your mind of clutter and keep you focused only on what is in front of you. Distractions, even if it is a reminder of something you "might" or "could" or "should" do later, take valuable energy away from your task at hand. Elite performers have no distractions. That is their edge over the competition.

➢ <u>Slower is faster.</u> Winners are relentless in finding ways to simplify, streamline, and get the job done right the first time. They are methodical and predictable. Instead of performing your duties at a faster pace, find ways to eliminate waste and inefficiency so you can keep the same, steady pace, yet complete your task in less time because you were able to cut out that which was not necessary for winning.

The *CATSHOT 13* process of identifying goals and making constant improvements is key to focusing your passion and harnessing your free will so that you will soon be on your way to your Noble Calling. *CATSHOT 13* helps you create a personal winning culture by focusing your efforts and taking you to the next level. It is an exhilarating process.

Our next chapter will bring all of these lessons together and help you better understand the impact the Performance Triad can have on your life.

Points to Remember

- *Focus* is the third and final element of the Performance Triad—the Heat. Without it, you will not ignite your passion and advance to the next level of performance.

- Building a **Personal Winning Culture** is important if you want to instill those habits that create world-class, elite performance.

> ➢ Embrace your free will.

> ➢ Know your limits and when and how to adjust them.

> ➢ Look out for team members.

> ➢ Watch out for so-called "experts."

> ➢ Clean jets fly better.

> ➢ Slower is faster.

POH Exercise

What are you going to focus on so that you can pursue your passion and achieve your Noble Calling?

Just like physical exercise helps build your body's muscles, mental exercises are necessary to build your intellectual muscle; most goals are primarily mental, even if the goal is to be physically fit.

Therefore, you now need to revisit your Noble Calling from Chapter 1 and your free will statements from Chapter 2 to develop the skills you will need to focus your efforts on achieving your goals.

The official *CATSHOT 13* POH has several in-depth exercises to help you with this. However, if you are working on your own (without the POH), ask yourself the questions below to determine how you can begin to use each of these characteristics of elite performers:

> ➢ Embrace your free will. What routine at work can you question? How can you work with your supervisors to revisit that routine and improve it?

> ➢ Know your limits and when and how to adjust them. What are the limits you will respect as you move toward accomplishing your goals?

> ➢ Look out for team members. What can you do for your team to bring them together?

> ➢ Watch out for so-called "experts." What outside experts do you rely on so much that you are not sure what they do? What can you do to learn more about their contribution, so you can better manage them or take over those duties?

> ➢ Clean jets fly better. Where can you clean up clutter, both physical and mental? At home and at work?

> ➢ Slower is faster. What process or task at work can you do in a more streamlined, methodical, and seemingly slower fashion in order to accomplish the process or task faster?

Write down your answers. You will revisit these answers

as you continue with the *CATSHOT 13* process and gauge your progress. You'll find this to be an important part of the accountability process.

(Note: We recommend you use the complete, detailed version of this POH exercise, which can be found on http://catshotgroup.com/productsservices/books, after you have completely read through this book.)

Chapter 4:

Maximizing Achievement—Your Personal Performance Triad

"**A**dmin," I said.

The room fell silent as I started the airshow debrief. Our Operations Officer, Blue Angel #5, went line-by-line over the rest of the day's and evening's schedules and events. Each person in the room took their turn to provide a quick self-assessment on how we did in achieving our specific goals for that airshow demonstration. We followed up by carefully dissecting the videotape of each maneuver.

With this process, we were doing what the best sport teams and business organizations do after training or an event. We were reviewing our performance, looking at every detail to see where we could improve the next time.

In this particular case, it was at the end of Blue Angel Winter training in El Centro, CA. We had just completed our very first airshow of the season in front of a live audience.

We had successfully transformed ourselves from a group of highly qualified fleet F/A-18 fighter pilots into a team of Blue Angel flight demonstration pilots. Every member of the support personnel had done their part as well.

The winter training process had taken roughly 13 weeks. To become a well-synchronized team, we each had to maximize our physical capabilities and excel in mentally preparing ourselves as we learned our new trade.

It was a hard but exhilarating experience to learn how to perform at such an extreme level. Each individual's passion for maximizing his or her performance and the Noble Calling of the mission kept us going, especially during the inevitable periods where performance plateaued or even temporarily slid backwards.

Although a lot of corporate knowledge was passed down from the last Blue Angel team, it still took considerable free will from each current team member to learn the techniques that worked for them in performing at such a high level.

Finally, it took dedicated focus to harness all of our passion and free will. A continuous assessment of individual progress and then total concentration on one or two areas that needed improving each day led to achievement at higher and higher levels.

From the crowd's perspective, that first show probably looked almost flawless.

But, in our debrief, we knew that it was just one step in a long journey. We were excited to have achieved our first 13-week milestone and to perform our first show. We were equally excited to launch our next 13-week cycle so we could improve on the many areas we found lacking during our debrief.

For the next 13 weeks, we would consider ourselves as still being newbies with a lot more to learn.

Passion, free will, and focus had worked synergistically to get us safely to this point. These elements gave us the needed momentum to propel us forward as individuals and as a team as we passionately worked at refining and improving the air show season.

Momentum and Your Personal Performance Triad

As you can see, the Performance Triad takes three strong aspects of success and makes them stronger by balancing them together. The momentum you get when that balance is reached is incredible! It creates a snowball effect that helps you continue to move toward your Noble Calling with greater and greater speed.

During this time, you begin to emanate an aura of success and develop a legacy that inspires those around you.

The purpose of creating and maintaining your personal Performance Triad is to build this momentum that will keep you relentlessly innovating and performing at higher and higher levels.

Your passion for what you do will fuel your constant effort to improve and innovate. You will live in this culture of excellence where your success will encourage you to raise your level of performance. Your enthusiasm will be contagious.

Yet, as with any process, you will need to find ways to measure your success. This will help you create specific goals on which to direct the efforts of your personal Performance Triad.

The Building-Block Approach: Measuring Your Success

Elite athletes, business leaders, and military professionals are great sources of inspiration as their record of achievement in their given occupation is well-documented by the media who love to report on wealth, awards, and other outside measures of success.

While these measurements should not be misconstrued as a goal or Noble Calling, they do provide a quantifiable snapshot of success for a particular moment in time. However, each of us must be our own judge on how well we achieved our ultimate goal, and whether we remained true to our Noble Calling.

Just like elite performers in any given field look for incremental improvements in a variety of areas, you will do the same with your *CATSHOT 13* POH.

CATSHOT 13 gives you tools to create those measurements, or building blocks, that will help you evaluate your progress daily and weekly as you go through the program. Some metrics can be objective and empirical such as fitness statistics, while others will be subjective such as your feelings of motivation.

Because this is an individually tailored program, you will need to create your own set of metrics customized for your use. It is fun and exhilarating to see your own progress in the various categories of health and fitness, personal skills, professional skills, and specific goal achievement.

While it is important to set goals, many people fail to set them properly. Each goal should be as specific as possible, be measurable, and include a time element. For example, "I want to lose weight" is not a good goal. "I want to lose 10 pounds and 3 inches off of my waist by Thanksgiving Day" is a great goal.

It is also important that you have short-, mid-, and long-term goals. You should start by setting the long-term goals, then creating the mid-term goals that lead to that, followed by the short-term goals that will get you started. The short-term goals may look more like a list of tasks. You will then begin to execute starting with the short-term goals and moving up to the long-term goals.

Here are some key questions to ask yourself along the way:

> ➢ <u>Long-Term or Life Goals</u> This is where you define your life and what you want it to mean. How do you want your biography to read? What do you want your legacy to be? What do you want to do for your family or your country before you die?

> ➢ <u>Interim or Annual Goals</u> Your annual career goals should go here—about one to three years out. What do you want to accomplish on the job or at school? How do you want your superiors and your peers to see you? What new skill do you want to acquire? What will you do that is new and unexpected? How will you impact your team, your company, and your industry?

> ➢ <u>Short-Term or 13-Weeks Out</u> These goals are often task oriented to support your broader goals. What are the steps you must take this week or this month that will help you achieve your interim and long-term goals? How can you do your job more efficiently and effectively? What processes can be improved? What targets can be expanded?

Optimizing Your Output

Just as a coach modifies the original training plan to maximize improvement as a team goes through a training camp, you will make adjustments to your program and your goals in order to maximize your learning curve as you progress.

The process is analogous to a modern automobile engine. Cars are designed to maximize output for a given amount of fuel by using computerized controls that continuously adjust the variables of fuel to air mixture, spark and valve timing for a given RPM, and power demands coming from your right foot.

Similarly, in *CATSHOT 13*, you will continually be searching for the right balance in your personal Performance Triad in order to advance your progress toward reaching your goals.

Stand By to Launch Yourself on an Exciting Mission!

One of the most frequent comments I get when discussing *CATSHOT 13* is regarding the sense of satisfaction, or fulfillment, clients get when they focus their efforts and align their passion, free will, and focus.

The muscle and brain memory gained and the process of improvement learned helps create an ever-lasting culture of achievement that individuals can continue to use throughout their lifetime. They get excited about the process. They enjoy it. I am confident that you will experience the same thing. Perhaps you have already had that feeling from something you have dedicated yourself to before. *CATSHOT 13* will rekindle that sense of satisfaction and reinvigorate the winning culture that already exists within you.

When you follow the program, you will have a clearer vision of what your Noble Calling is. You will be healthier in mind, body, and spirit. You will have improved personal and professional skills. You will be expanding your frontier of human performance. These elements alone will be exciting.

Even more exciting is that you will also have a higher sense of what living with passion is really like. You will have a clearer vision of what you want, where you are going, and how you are going to get there. Once you reach that point, you will never consider what you are doing "work" again. It is a passionate pursuit of your ultimate goal. Your Noble Calling!

Let's get ready to launch!

Points to Remember

- The *Performance Triad* requires constant attention to the balancing of your Passion, Free Will, and Focus in order to reach optimal success.

- The building-block approach of measuring in small steps your achievement and progress toward your goals, which are aligned with your Noble Calling, helps you to maintain your personal Performance Triad balance.

- The *CATSHOT 13* process includes creating specific, measurable goals with time limits. It is important that you are able to measure and visualize your progress so that you can stay motivated and relentlessly innovate and improve; never stop measuring and re-measuring your progress.

POH Exercise

Visual Representation of Your Plan

Now take the information you have developed so far and, using abbreviated terms if necessary, fill in the achievements next to each heading. Then take this same data and fill it in on your *CATSHOT 13* plan in pencil. (Don't worry if it is not perfect, you will review this document at least once a week, and you will be encouraged to make adjustments as necessary as you refine your vision.)

Achievements

Noble Calling _____

Interim Goals

1. _____

2. _____

3. _____

CATSHOT 13 **Goals**

1. _____

2. _____

3. _____

Work top to bottom to develop your plan. Work bottom to top to execute your plan.

See the detailed version of this planning exercise in the POH at http://catshotgroup.com/productsservices/books.

Section 2:

"Hand Salute"

Take the *CATSHOT*, Launch, Achieve, and Win!

Sitting in the cockpit of my multi-million-dollar F/A-18 strike fighter on the deck of the USS Dwight D. Eisenhower (CVN 69), I can feel the vibration and hear the hum as I power up my engines.

Imagine you are with me in the jet. Only a "holdback" mechanism links our aircraft to the flight deck, preventing us from moving, until the steam pressure reaches the pressure needed to launch.

The rest of the team is moving around the flight deck in a well-choreographed ballet of humans and machines. We are all on a mission. We have the same goal: safely connect our aircraft to the catapult and shoot it off the deck and into the sky by combining hundreds of seamless and efficient movements in an exact sequence.

Everyone is in alignment. Our Performance Triads have been honed so that individually, and as a group, we are ready for virtually any and all scenarios.

We check our flight controls and instruments one more time, and when everything is ready, we look to the catapult officer who is standing clear of our aircraft off to the side. You give him a hand salute.

The catapult officer makes his absolute final check and gives the signal to launch to the catapult operator who fires the catapult, taking us from a dead stop to 150 knots, or 173 mph, almost instantly.

The acceleration slams your whole body into the back of the ejection seat in one swift, consistent motion. It does not stop until … Bam! … The catapult slams into its breaking mechanism at the end of the deck. We are shot forward, set free. We are flying.

That is the CATSHOT!

Until this moment, everything was just preparation. Now, we are on the move.

* * *

For the next 13 weeks, your *CATSHOT 13* program will teach you skills to create your own building-block approach to achieving success as you define it; this could be improved health, increased income, or enhanced relationships.

Now that you understand the Performance Triad and the importance of balancing your passion, free will, and focus, we will move on to the power of the launch. You will sense an incredible CATSHOT of acceleration in achievement as you use the foundation of your personal Performance Triad to plan, continually improve, embrace challenge and opportunities, and develop a life plan for excellence.

In the following chapters, we are going to introduce you to a proven training plan, similar to what is used by the Blue Angels and TOPGUN in training their elite aviators. You will find that it can just as easily work for you too.

Let's launch!

Chapter 5:

Your Inspired Plan— CATSHOT 13

Welcome to your own personal Jet Camp.

This is the chapter you will bookmark and return to again and again. It is by far the longest and most detailed. It is here that we get into the meat of the program!

You are about to dedicate yourself in the same manner as the elite professionals who prepare to tackle their own big, professional goals.

Just like these top performers, *CATSHOT 13* will help you build up to your big goal by first focusing on the smaller, individual components necessary to achieve that goal. This building-block approach can be found in the Blue Angel winter training, baseball spring training, and even in medical residence training. They all use a similar format to meet the powerful demands of their professions. It works, it is safe, and it minimizes risk.

This 13-week program aligns itself to the four seasons of the year, the four quarters of a business calendar, and to many school years. My personal experience has shown again and again that 13 weeks is the amount of time it takes to go from zero to a reasonable level of mastery for just about any skill.

To move to a higher level, we will go through another 13-week period, then another, and another.

Because this program has been proven time and time again, you can have faith that it will help you achieve your goals too. The process you are about to embark on came from years of proven methodologies in teaching the best fighter pilots in the world, and in the case of the Blue Angels, performing the most extreme flight demonstrations of any jet demo team.

Going for It! Building Your Own Personal Culture to Win

Winning in life involves attacking the issues found in each step we take toward our goals, and overcoming the obstacles in our path. This is not a one-time effort. It is a way of life and of looking at how you can achieve far beyond your expectations.

The plan involves identifying your goals, creating a strategy to reach them, building the skills necessary to overcome the surprises, and being so committed to the end goal — your Noble Calling — that you continually improve your processes.

The elite players in any field are what we call Relentless Innovators. They are the people in your office, or your community, or on your team who are never satisfied. They always want to improve and change the way things are done.

For example, if your team sold a record 10 widgets this year, the Relentless Innovators will want to sell 12 and may even look for ways to cut 10% off of the cost of making the widget. If you use beef in your chili recipe, they use beef, veal, and pork and are constantly playing with the ratios of beef to veal to pork so they can win the neighborhood cook-off. They are always moving and changing, taking in information, digesting it, and applying it.

CATSHOT 13 consists of the 13 steps, explained below, which you will follow every 13 weeks. This proven methodology breaks down each goal into easy-to-accomplish tasks, with each task building on the one before.

While you could just jump into the CATSHOT 13 POH and begin — it is reasonably self-explanatory — I highly recommend that you take the time to read through the following pages to see the big picture before you start. Along the way, we will provide important tips that will help you successfully complete the program and build on your new-found capabilities.

Step 1: Determine Your Noble Calling

You may recall from Chapter 1, that your *Noble Calling* is your ultimate purpose in life. It is the "true north" for all of your life goals, both personal and professional. This is what drives you to perform, to overcome obstacles, and to sacrifice instant gratification for long-term success.

What do you want people to say at a cocktail party when they are referring to you? How will people eulogize you when you are gone? We want you to try to pinpoint the essence of who you are, or who you would like to be.

This is not a list of accomplishments, rather an overarching description of who you are. Most of you just starting your *CATSHOT 13* program will likely find this a very daunting first step.

The beauty of this program is that you will be going back through it over and over again, improving your answers and honing your focus each time.

Think of all of the intellectual goals and physical activities that make you feel exhilarated. Consider what they have in common to determine what is at the core of your being.

You should set aside at least one hour of uninterrupted time to contemplate these questions. Reaching the level of world-class players takes time, effort, and commitment. It will not be achieved in one afternoon.

This is the step where you determine the "why" in your life. Why do you get out of bed every morning and keep moving? Your Noble Calling is your foundation.

Step 2: Determine Your Intermediate and Yearly Goals

Write down the life goals that seem like logical steps along the path to you achieving your Noble Calling. Begin with a yearly goal; then outline the steps or intermediate goals that will get you there. All of your goals and plans will be based on the best assumptions and facts that you have at the present time. Include measureable results and a timeline within each goal.

For example, if your Noble Calling is to help humanity by supporting your country, you may want to join a branch of the U. S. military or the U.S. Department of State. Your assumption should be that you can reach a position and provide a skill that makes you an asset to those organizations that will lead to a safer, stronger, and more productive nation. One of the logical intermediate goals to accomplish this may be to lose 10 pounds so you can pass the physical.

Or maybe your Noble Calling is to be the family patriarch and help future generations of your family flourish. Your intermediate goal may then be to support your family and send your children to quality schools. This may require you to increase your sales by 10%, thus increasing your sales bonus in order to pay for the tuition.

Goals are the frame of your life that sits on the foundation. Goals are much stronger and easier to accomplish when you tie them back to the "why" in your life.

If you are completely blank on a Noble Calling, do not let that stop you from starting your *CATSHOT 13* process; nothing should stop you!

Since you will be revising each of these steps, you can begin with those goals that have been gnawing at you. By listing them and following these steps, you will begin to see patterns form. When you begin the next 13-week cycle, you will be that much closer to finding or more clearly identifying your Noble Calling.

Step 3: Determine Your *CATSHOT 13* Tasks

We are now putting the bricks onto the frame — the daily tasks that build, one on top of the other. This is where you break down the intermediate and annual goals into the steps necessary to get you there.

Select two to three goals that will be your focus for the next 13 weeks. Next, you need to add timeframes and measurable milestones to monitor your progress. This will keep you accountable and inspire you as you see visible progress.

If you continue to struggle with your Noble Calling — either you just do not have the direction or your cannot put your finger on it — you can focus your efforts on preparing yourself with the health and general life or business skills that will help you tackle a broad range of passions that you may be considering.

For example, you may want to take classes to learn more about a subject you think may be your calling, but you are not sure. You may want to try a new sport or try your hand at writing a book, even if it seems intimidating.

Step 4: Develop Your Building-Block Training Approach

Each task that moves you toward each goal that leads you to your Noble Calling can be categorized in the following areas: health, personal skills, and professional skills.

You should now take the goals and tasks you have developed and place them in the appropriate category. This will help you determine the building blocks necessary to move all areas of your life in the same direction.

For example, if you want to improve your physical health so you can perform better at work, this will impact your routines with family and your work. If you need to find time to exercise or change the way your family shops at the grocery store, others will be impacted and must be taken into consideration when developing your new plans.

By categorizing each task, you will see how it impacts each area, and this will help you to identify any conflicts that need to be resolved. For example, if you want to exercise more and spend more time with your family, then you may need to develop a plan for the family to do something more active together.

This is the point where you will begin to create a reasonable growth path to attaining your goals.

Step 5: Develop a Weekly Battle Rhythm That Works for You

Now we will begin to create good life habits.

Committing to become world-class and to follow your Noble Calling means that you will need to make changes to your daily life. You are choosing to change direction and to align with that which you have determined to be your true life meaning.

Therefore, you need to work out what your Weekly Battle Rhythm will be. I recommend starting with the following plan, and altering it to fit the realities of your personal schedule.

- **Monday through Friday,** execute your daily schedule, developed in Step 6.

- **Saturday**, execute your daily plan, and add to it a debrief from the previous week. Adjust your weekly goals as necessary based on what you have learned.

- **Sunday**, a rest day. Recharge. Prepare to hit it hard on Monday.

Step 6: Develop Your Daily Schedule

Changing habits is hard. I developed the following plan to stay focused on my goals and establish new, healthier habits. These moments of focus will help you stay on track as you work to form the new habits that will bring you closer to being true to your Noble Calling.

- **Morning visualization:**
  - o Visualize your Noble Calling—your Passion.
  - o Visualize your goals and the steps you are now taking toward them.
  - o Visualize your burning desire for your *CATSHOT 13* plan to succeed.

- **Review the schedule for the day:**
  - o Lay out the major events.
  - o Give yourself enough breaks to recharge.

- **Your schedule should include personal training in the following focus areas:**
  - o Your health: mind, body, and spirit
  - o Your personal life skills

    o Your professional skills

- **Set your specific goal for the day:**

    o Identify the one area you had the most difficulty with over the last few days.

    o Visualize success here, and focus your efforts on it.

- **Execute the day:**

    o Take notes in your *CATSHOT 13* notebook on how you are doing.

    o Give yourself a check mid-day, to see if you need to adjust your day's tasks.

    o Keep your notes and records together for your weekly debrief, as well as to monitor your progress over the 13-week period.

- **Debrief the day and determine your plan to improve tomorrow:**

    o Go down your checklist of tasks and your specific goals for the day.

    o Be honest in assessing your performance.

    o Pick one goal that will be your specific goal for tomorrow.

   o Go to sleep with a positive attitude visualizing yourself successfully achieving your specific goal.

Step 7: Determine Your Metrics for Success

As management guru Peter Drucker said, "What gets measured gets managed."

In other words, if we can measure something—whether it is pounds lost, widgets sold, dinners at home with the family—we are more likely to pay attention to that number and work to improve it. General comments such as "doing more" are often ignored, or worse, measured by different standards by different people, which leads to disappointment.

Next to each of your goals, your tasks, and even your building blocks (Steps 2, 3, and 4), write down a method of measuring them. Then write down the timeline for achieving those measurements.

These measurements must be meaningful and well thought out to ensure you are getting the most from your training. You will then determine the timeline for achieving milestones, and write those dates on your calendar for tracking.

The more specific the measurements, milestones, and dates, the better. Breaking down each of these tasks into the smallest piece as possible can really be motivating.

For example, if you want to sell 10 more widgets this year, then that is one every 36.5 days. If you make a sale for every 10 calls you make, then you need to make 10 calls in 36.5 days or one every 3 to 4 days. If you go 10 days without a sales call, then you will realize quickly that you need to turn up the heat by making more calls. You might also consider ways to become more efficient in your sales calls, so you increase your close rate. Either way, by breaking down your tasks, you can quickly recognize when you need to adjust your behavior, rather than waiting until year's end when you do not have enough time to catch up.

Step 8: Periodically Adjust Your Plan

When you get to your milestones, you will be prompted to periodically review the facts and assumptions you made when you originally developed your *CATSHOT 13* program. Changing facts or incorrect assumptions can be expected. Even with the best planning, we just get it wrong.

For example, maybe after more research and exposure, you find you do not like working in government at all, and another path would be better for you. Or, perhaps you determined that selling more widgets did not improve the bottom line as much as making them more efficiently will. Also, the people around us do not always have our same goals, and thus can change the game board on us. You should always be prepared to alter your course.

When you find that the facts and assumptions have changed, you will need to review and reassess your goals and tasks and adjust accordingly. This is all part of your weekly Battle Rhythm's debriefing session. Making little adjustments as you go is much more efficient and effective than waiting until the end of the year and possibly having to completely change direction.

Step 9: Create Your Personal Standard Operating Procedures

Just like fighter pilots, your personal Standard Operating Procedures (SOP) will be one of your greatest assets when it comes to developing high achievement muscle and brain memory.

The more processes that you can make routine and write down in such a manner that anyone could pick up your manual and do it without your direction, the better off you will be. For example, your billing process should run like clockwork with the same type of info on all of the invoices, the invoices going out on the same day each month, and with the same double-checks in place, ensuring that the money has arrived.

These basic standards will allow you to focus on execution at a very high level without having to worry about reinventing the wheel and briefing someone else on all the small details every time you conduct an evolution.

Your SOP will also be one of your weapons against goal creep and other enemies to your success. It will help you avoid relearning many of the lessons other successful people have learned the hard way in the past. Additionally, we will discuss how and when you should review and change the personalized SOP items you develop in a calculated, evolutionary approach.

Your personal SOP is a key element to your success. Therefore, it will be covered in greater detail in later chapters.

Step 10: Create Your Own List of Operating Limitations and Boldface Emergency Procedures

As in many professional occupations, fighter pilots have standardized limitations on how they operate their aircraft and conduct their personal business. For example, we have minimums on such things as the amount of rest and sleep we must have between flights and maximums on such things as our consumption of alcohol.

Aviation is very unforgiving. When things go wrong and an aircraft malfunction occurs, pilots must react quickly to achieve their goal of making it home safely. To improve their chances, they memorize emergency procedures that are outlined in the flight manuals in boldface print and they execute them as soon as a problem develops.

Like the SOP and "boldface procedures," these limits and steps were developed for the fighter pilot community to prevent loss of life or loss of an aircraft. Unless you are flying fighters, driving race cars, or climbing mountains, your *CATSHOT 13* program is not likely designed to operate in as extreme an environment.

Yet, whether you are a school teacher, a stock broker, or an entrepreneur, your list of personal limitations and boldface procedures will help prevent things like physical injury and sickness, which can knock you off track and put you behind on your goals.

Therefore, your personal list of limitations and emergency procedure steps that you develop will be critical to your success.

Step 11: Execute Your Personal Accountability Process

Personal accountability is one of the critical processes in your ability to expand your achievement.

You must be brutally honest as you conduct self-evaluation throughout each 13-week period. Briefing and debriefing techniques will be discussed in the following chapters, and instructions to download a free copy of the daily planning sheets from the POH will be made available to you.

These briefs and debriefs have applications in all areas where performance matters: teaching, athletics, business, medicine, and the military, to name a few.

The metrics you developed in Step 7 will be very important here. During this process, you must ensure that the metric you chose actually measures the behavior you wanted to target and change.

For example, you may think you want to lose 10 pounds, when your goal is really to be more fit. You might determine that improving your time when running or increasing the number of reps you can perform of an exercise while maintaining good form are really better measures than weight loss. In order to realize this, you must be brutally honest about whether your measurements are helping you reach your goal, or if they are just an easy checklist item for you.

In these next chapters, you will be introduced to the same method used by TOPGUN instructors to evaluate your own performance. TOPGUN participants are encouraged to stay positive and to speak about their performance and challenges in a positive manner.

Similarly, you will be introduced to the accountability method used by the Blue Angels, such as "safeties" and the "five-dollar rule." This keeps things serious, but also fun.

For example, an individual Blue Angel will call a "safety" on themselves when an SOP or limitation has been violated during a practice, an actual demonstration, or while on personal time away from the team. The penalty is to pay five dollars into a kitty for later use by the team.

Accountability is not about a "gotcha" moment pointed out by someone else, but more about calling yourself out so you can improve. Oftentimes, you may be the only person who knows where you fell short. It is very important that you can recognize these moments.

Step 12: Select Coaches and Training Partners

Coaches can be a valuable asset. So can training partners. Used at the right times, they can accelerate your CATSHOT process.

However, the wrong coach or training partner, or a good coach or training partner chosen for the wrong reasons, will be detrimental to your progress. Therefore, you need to be careful, and brutally honest with yourself, when choosing a coach or training partner.

There is a significant difference in the mentality of a coach who is charged with bringing together a team as opposed to one who is charged with enhancing one particular individual's performance. The best coaches can do both, but not all possess this skill. It is important to choose the type of coach you need, not just a friend who is available.

All successful individuals have learned how to be their own coaches as a check and balance to outside coaches. No matter how good a coach is, only you will truly know your passion and Noble Calling. Therefore, just like choosing a business partner or a spouse, selecting a coach or training partner is a very serious decision.

We will discuss how to assess who is the best coach or training partner for you in a later chapter.

Step 13: Celebrate Your Win!

Celebrating your success is the final step of the *CATSHOT 13* program.

It is important at the end of each 13-week program to acknowledge your accomplishments. Even if you fall short of achieving your goals, you may see that you still made exceptional progress. Part of the process is having fun and fueling your passion to keep going. So take a positive approach, celebrate what you did accomplish, and take advantage of the opportunity to do it smarter and better the next time!

Seeing your progress and recognizing your role in making it happen will inspire you to go through the 13-week process again and again.

It will be your responsibility to start a new *CATSHOT 13* as soon as possible! This renewed dedication will elevate your spirit and push you to achieve even more.

* * *

Remember: This is *your* plan. In the end, you are responsible for making sure it is executed with enthusiasm and that you are honest with yourself in order to move forward. Our next chapter will help you take charge of your *CATSHOT 13*!

Points to Remember

Step 1: Determine Your Noble Calling

Step 2: Determine Your Intermediate and Yearly Goals

Step 3: Determine Your *CATSHOT 13* Tasks

Step 4: Develop Your Building-Block Training Approach

Step 5: Develop a Weekly Battle Rhythm That Works for You

Step 6: Develop Your Daily Schedule

Step 7: Determine Your Metrics for Success

Step 8: Periodically Adjust Your Plan

Step 9: Create Your Personal Standard Operating Procedures

Step 10: Create Your Own List of Operating Limitations and Boldface Emergency Procedures

Step 11: Execute Your Personal Accountability Process

Step 12: Select Coaches and Training Partners

Step 13: Celebrate Your Win!

POH Exercise

Start with the pre-formatted pages found in the *CATSHOT 13* POH located on http://catshotgroup.com/products services/books, or create your own version. You'll need 13 sheets of paper for your first cycle. At the top of each page, write down one of the steps so that you end up with a separate sheet of paper for each step. You will want a new set of pages for each time you repeat the 13-week plan.

For your very first 13-week program, you will go one step at a time and write down all of your thoughts about that step. Once you have answered all of the questions in the POH and written everything you can think of, you will move to the next page for the next step, and so on. This will help you better understand the *CATSHOT 13* program and how each step leads you to the next.

For subsequent 13-week cycles, you will want to do the same thing, but this time, make notes in the next cycle's steps based on your experience with the current cycle.

For example, in your first 13-week program, you may not have determined your Noble Calling, so you might have written something like "improve health and business rela-tionships." As you work your way through the first cycle, you may start to see patterns, such as you want to teach people about health or you want to serve your country. Instead of stopping your first 13-week cycle to start over with this new information, you will make those notes on the pages for the next cycle while you continue to refine your thinking. Therefore, in the next 13-week cycle, you will already have those thoughts and assumptions to take under consideration as you move forward.

In other words, you do not want to keep interrupting the current 13-week cycle to start over. "Chasing the next shiny object" so to speak is inefficient. You want to methodically finish one cycle and then improve on the next go around. Being very deliberate is the key to efficiency! Changes need to be well thought out!

Chapter 6:

The Power of Being Your Own Coach— Continuous Improvement

Being Your Own Technical Coach

"A little pull ... a little more pull ... a little more pullll," I said in a slow, steady cadence as I completed the Delta Roll profile at our winter training facility in El Centro, CA.

The five other pilots, all in gleaming F/A-18 fighter jets like mine, were flying just inches away. We were learning to roll all six of our aircraft safely with me in the lead. Unlike what I expected after reading and following the notes from my predecessor, I had to command a lot more pulls on the control stick than what was documented in the plan.

What was I doing wrong?

My right wingman and my slot pilot, both of whom had flown with the previous "Boss" the year before I took the helm, were equally perplexed. We were flying the prescribed profile at the right airspeeds and roll rates, but it just was not working out. I was completing my rolls too low to the ground and we had to pull more Gs to avoid scraping the desert floor.

In our building-block training plan, we had just started working on the Delta Formation. This formation required all six Blue Angel jets to fly together like a flock of geese with a stinger if you will, a big triangle going through the sky.

During the normal show sequence, the team comes together into the Delta Formation near the end of the performance. However, because we were working on part-task training, we were dedicating an entire flight on just that last portion of the show — the Delta Formation maneuvers.

My wingmen were getting justifiably annoyed as I continued to need more than the prescribed number of pulls during these Delta maneuvers. As much as they tried, the team could not identify what I was doing wrong. All they knew was that I was not doing it like the last Boss. I was setting back the progress in our training plan.

After several days of this, I started analyzing it more on my own. I really had to think. I noticed that midway through our practice, when our jets had burned down to the same fuel weight that they would be at during a normal airshow, the maneuver worked as advertised in my pass down.

Bingo! I had figured out the issue.

I discussed it with my team. We agreed that when we were doing the Delta Roll sequence in practice, we were at a heavier fuel weight than in the airshow. Therefore, we would have to add more airspeed at the start of the maneuver to make up the difference. This would still allow the roll rate and G forces to be similar to the real show.

We were back on track.

The lesson I took from that experience was this: My experienced wingmen, who were acting as my coaches, had never been presented with this situation before. The previous Boss had figured it out, and just made up the difference without mentioning anything to the team. To him, it was second nature. To me, in my first year as the Boss, it was not. And all my wingmen knew was that my roll was not like the previous Boss's roll.

Therefore, I had to be my own coach.

* * *

Throughout my Naval Aviation career, no matter how experienced my flight leads, mentors, or wingmen were, it was often up to me to figure out the best way to accomplish my task.

This same concept holds true in other occupations. There will always come a time when you have to take as much input as you can from others, analyze it, and then figure it out for yourself.

This especially holds true for finding your passion in life and your Noble Calling. No one will know you better than you. So, the sooner you develop the skills necessary to take input from your coach or other advisors, analyze them, and then make your own determination as to what will get you closer to your Noble Calling, the better off you will be.

Sports teams need coaches to bring individuals together to function as a unit. When you are working on your personal human achievement, coaches can be valuable. However, finding your passion and determining your Noble Calling must be your responsibility.

Being Your Own Life Coach

Coaching is not about knowing how to perform a task better than those whom you are coaching. Coaching is about being able to see the big picture and understanding each task, so that you can direct those on your team to use their individual skills to move across the goal line together.

This is why you must be your own life coach. Only you can see the big picture. Only you know what tasks and skills are needed to reach your goals. Only you are focused on your Noble Calling.

Input from others, particularly those who are strong where you are weak, is great. You should reach out to those you admire, or at least study them and emulate their best behaviors. However, in the end, you must make the final call on the direction your life takes.

Ford, Edison, Gates, and Jobs all dropped out of high school or college. I am sure someone told them to stay in school! For many, such as medical doctors or lawyers, school is required to follow that passion. Yet for others it may not be necessary. You must decide what is right for you.

The Power of Visualization

Visualization—the act of picturing yourself achieving your goal—is a time-proven technique in sports, business, and the military. This technique is critical to improving your technical skills and helping warm up your muscle and brain memory before a critical event.

At the Blue Angels, we would "chair fly" the entire flight demonstration during our pre-flight briefing to warm us up. Long before we touched the actual aircraft controls, we were mimicking the movements in a chair, closing our eyes and envisioning ourselves in flight.

In many self-help books, the term "auto suggestion" or the phrase "thoughts are things" are used to describe this concept and the importance of visualizing your future outcomes. Just like an athlete visualizes himself or herself winning the trophy before a competition, you must visualize yourself living out your Noble Calling, following your passion, achieving whatever it is in terms of wealth and success that you desire. It is a powerful tool that works.

Long before I became a TOPGUN instructor or a Blue Angel, I dreamed of achieving both of those coveted positions. I would visualize my 1966 Corvette, which I bought dirt-cheap and fixed up, sitting in the parking lots of TOPGUN and the Blue Angels' base.

Imaging that! I found myself a member of both squadrons later on. Coincidence? I don't think so.

That visualization was just one of many similar scenarios I thought myself through. I prepared myself mentally, by imagining I was already there as a member of both teams. It is not magic. In each case, the visualizations worked on my subconscious, and I began doing the things I needed to do to make those visualizations reality.

The *CATSHOT 13* program trains you to visualize your Noble Calling every day, as well as the specific tasks you need to accomplish to reach it. It does not need to be a long process, just a few minutes. As you gain experience with visualization, you will understand how integral these techniques are to the building block training approach. It is also part of being your own coach and being very deliberate about your development.

Deliberate Training

All successful individuals make an effort to improve themselves every day. The most successful are very deliberate with their focus and the methods they use. You will also find that these individuals always try to make the process fun and motivational.

The process of improving is one of the most exciting parts of the *CATSHOT 13* program. This is true for any occupation, even those that are deadly serious—like being a fighter pilot, a surgeon, a firefighter, or a Navy SEAL.

Part of being your own coach is being able to determine the best training regimen that will work for you.

If you are in an occupation that already has a training plan, you will accelerate your results, and also the results of your team, when you develop an inspirational personal training program that fits within the institutionalized one. *CATSHOT 13* will guide you through the process of developing your personal, deliberate, and innovative training plan.

Briefing

Critical to success at both the macro and micro levels of execution is briefing for the event ahead of time.

High risk occupations such as being a fighter pilot, a surgeon, or running an oil drilling rig all rely on pre-mission briefings to help warm up the muscle and brain memory. They also identify hazards and potential barriers to success, map out a winning game plan, and then visualize what success looks like.

In my consulting business, I often see poor performance and inefficient execution. I can trace most of it back to incoherent or non-existent pre-mission briefings.

CATSHOT 13 will provide you with an easy-to-use and efficient briefing format. It will be one of the key elements to successfully executing specific tasks within your daily and weekly routines and, ultimately, your overall personal *CATSHOT 13* program.

The process of briefing for your plan includes not only developing your own plan, but also considering all of the potential moves by your "adversary," and then practicing your counters to those moves. In some cases, such as in sports, business, or politics, your adversary will be a competitor. But what we are really talking about here are those people, things, or events that have influence on your ability to achieve your goals and follow your Noble Calling.

Within our recommended briefing format, you will identify your performance categories and your specific goal for the evolution, and you will visualize the critical elements necessary for success. You will also rehearse your boldface emergencies, which we mentioned in an earlier chapter and will discuss further in Chapter 7.

This should be part of your personal culture of excellence. It is definitely part of being your own coach.

To the uninitiated, a briefing before beginning the work sounds redundant, time-consuming, and like a lot of effort.

Actually, these briefings have proven to take less time, be more efficient, and achieve better results in the long run because, in the end, fewer mistakes are made in the execution. Mistakes take time to fix.

The value of visualization in a pre-mission brief cannot be understated. As the Blue Angel "Boss," or the flight leader, I led the team through a visualization exercise before every flight and before each practice.

It was the same scenario from the very first day on the job until my last performance two years and hundreds of practices and airshows later. To accomplish it, we would sit in our briefing room and pretend to manipulate the controls of our aircraft and think through our routines. We adjusted for the anticipated weather and environment. It worked every time.

Additionally, each person involved in the brief would identify his or her specific goal for that evolution. Usually, it was to correct a deficiency that they themselves identified on a previous event. When you pay particular attention to one item and visualize the corrective action and proper outcome, your learning curve increases and your performance accelerates. It is a powerful combination!

Whether you are preparing for a business negotiation or coaching your child's soccer team, when you take the time to brief your plan, your overall execution will improve dramatically.

Debriefing — Remembering the Fight and Taking Good Notes

To new fighter pilots, the combat arena can be extremely disorienting. It seems like you are surrounded by a swarm of high performance aircraft that are all trying to kill you!

You are often at the edge of consciousness as you sustain nearly eight or nine times the force of gravity in your maneuvers. Your aircraft shudders as it strains at the limits of its capability, often to the point where the gauges are difficult to read. The sun, clouds, and the Earth are all spinning around. You are hot and uncomfortable with sweat dripping in your eyes. Keeping track of what is going on is difficult.

Maintaining situation awareness, as we call it, is a challenge. Often pilots returning for the post-mission debrief could not tell you one thing that happened correctly — learning and improving is next to impossible in that circumstance. Because of this, we always focused on trying to reconstruct the entire air-to-air engagement from start to finish.

What we witnessed was, as fighter pilots gained experience, they learned to take accurate notes of what happened in an engagement — not an easy task when you are trying to fly your airplane at the same time.

After a while, students were able to recall the entire fight and the important details in their heads with no notes at all.

Airspeeds, altitudes, directions of turns, loops, pirouettes, position of the sun and clouds—all were important. Most importantly, what was the enemy aircraft doing and were you on or off your game plan?

At TOPGUN, we saw dramatic improvements in performance when a young fighter pilot could remember those parameters.

The same debriefing techniques are used in sports. Amazingly, at least in my years of experience working with various business leaders, formal debriefing is rarely used. Whether after a negotiation, a sales pitch to a customer, or a manufacturing evolution, a lethargic pace of improvement is all you will ever see if those involved do not debrief important events as a matter of personal and organizational culture.

Often, those in charge do not want to be told they did poorly, nor do they want to confront individual employees. It is much easier to hand out general comments to the team. However, this leaves no one accountable for errors, and no plans for improvement developed. The same holds true for you personally!

At TOPGUN, we tried to avoid this issue by always debriefing in the third person. We took the "who" out of it. We would say that the "fighter" made a mistake when he decided to reverse his turn as opposed to "you" made the mistake. From the instructor's vantage, we would say "the bandit" then took advantage of the situation and closed in for the kill shot, instead of "I shot you." In other words, we used "fighter" and "bandit" instead of "you" or "I." This helped keep the ego and emotion out of the discussion as much as possible while still getting the learning points across to the right people.

TOPGUN also used a "goods and others" scoring methodology for the same reason. It is also why we scored things in the most positive way. We would list the items to be scored vertically on the whiteboard. We would then make two columns, one for "goods," another for "others." The instructor would then proceed to summarize the debrief by scoring each item as either a "good" or an "other." How far to the left or how far to the right determined how good or how "other than good" the student did.

Through the *CATSHOT 13* program, you will learn how to "remember the fight," take good notes, and keep a positive mindset throughout the debrief by using the "goods and others" format. You will become a better coach to yourself and you will see improvements in your execution and achievement.

Honesty in your self-assessment will be critical as you work on being your own coach. My experience is that most people are harder on themselves than they are on others. So you will be encouraged to keep it fun with your personal $5 rule as you make mistakes and safeties. As your passion for perfection grows in your heart, you will see your performance metrics improve (while the dollar amount in the kitty decreases).

In any learning process, you will experience performance peaks, plateaus, and valleys. To deal with this, one of the critical skills you will learn is how to handle those inevitable situations so that your overall trend is up, like an aircraft's flight path at the end of a CATSHOT.

Points to Remember

- It is important that you participate in your own coaching program, even as you reach out to others who can help you strengthen those areas in which you are weakest.

- Visualizing yourself achieving your goals and living your Noble Calling is an important tool for setting the pace and the milestones to reach them.

- Honesty in your self-evaluation is key to your success.

- Train yourself to improve at least one skill every day; always move forward toward your specific goal.

- Brief yourself every day on what you plan to accomplish, and debrief after every major project or milestone in order to refine ways to constantly improve yourself.

POH Exercise

- Begin to list and measure your progress toward your goals and the tasks leading you there.

    o Pull out your weekly list of specific goals you set for your *CATSHOT 13* program.

    o List the specific tasks you need to achieve each of those goals with six or more small columns to the right of each one.

    o Use a metric scale that makes sense for you, either a "goods and others" format, or a 0 through 5 format.

    o Check the column with your progress or level of success next to each goal.

    o Note where most checks are—closer to "0" or closer to "5."

    o Revisit this every week to see if you are making progress.

- Visualize yourself achieving your goals. What does it look like?

    o On a sheet of paper, write down notes on what each goal looks like when successfully achieved. This will help you understand what it will take for you to feel like you have successfully accomplished the task and/or reached the goal.

- Create Briefing and Debriefing Sheets that support your goals and their tasks.

  o Write each of your goals across the top of a sheet of paper with the associated tasks or steps to reaching that goal.

  o Begin by writing "Briefing" under the first goal, and describe how you plan to achieve it.

  o Visualize yourself achieving the goal.

  o After you have worked on the goal, come back and write "Debriefing" under the "Briefing" section, and describe what happened when you actually attempted the goal or task.

    - What did you do right?

    - What could you have done better?

    - Where you successful?

    - If you need to make another pass at the goal, what do you plan to do differently?

Note: For examples of Briefing and Debriefing sheets, please see the POH, which can be found on our website at http://catshotgroup.com/productsservices/books.

Chapter 7:

Dog Fight Like a Fighter Pilot—
Embrace Challenge & Opportunity

You Fight Like You Train, So Learn to Drive the Fight

"Fights on!" the newbie pilot yelled over the radio.

"Trigger down . . . snap shot," I fired back. "Missed high."

This was the first head-on pass of a one-on-one practice dogfighting engagement for our new TOPGUN recruits. I was the instructor simulating a "bandit" in an old 1970s MiG-21. The student was the "fighter" in a brand new F/A-18 Hornet with all the bells and whistles.

We had started out heading in the exact same direction at 1.5-miles abeam, at 18,000 feet altitude with an airspeed of over 450 miles per hour. At the "fights on" call, we both selected full afterburner and turned toward each other for a head on pass. In this case, the bandit surprised the fighter with a harder pull and an aggressive early reversal move. The bandit then pulled lead just before the first merge and squeezed the 20MM cannon trigger in an attempt to make a simulated guns snapshot, spraying bullets from the fighter's nose to his tail as they passed each other at 900 miles per hour and only 500 feet apart.

The bandit was driving the fight. The fighter immediately recognizing his mistake, and before the bullets hit, rolled inverted and pulled hard to execute a nose-low guns defense. The bullets missed high. I hoped the fighter would learn and start driving the fight himself, making the bandit react to him.

If the fighter failed in this scenario, he would lose to an opponent with only a fraction of the hardware and software.

At TOPGUN, my fellow instructors and I would teach our students to "drive the fight." You had to understand the capabilities and limitations of your aircraft weapons system as well as your opponent's system. You would then craft a game plan to take advantage of your strengths and to exploit your opponent's weaknesses.

In practice, the instructors would simulate enemy fighters, or "bandits," often flying aircraft inferior in capability to what the student was flying. Most often, the bandit, even with his inferior equipment, would quickly gain advantage. The reason was that the "bandit-instructor, with his extensive experience advantage, was able to drive the fight.

Over time, the students learned to make aggressive moves that would force the bandit to react the way the fighter wanted him to react. As the bandit maneuvered to avoid getting shot, he would quickly become defensive, rather than offensive. The combination of being defensive and flying inferior machinery would result in the bandit's simulated death.

* * *

We know that in real combat, fighter pilots fight like they were trained. This has been proven time and again. It is also true in life.

You are going to execute the life skills and technical skills in the real world just as you execute them in *CATSHOT 13*. Therefore, you need to develop the muscle and brain memory in a way that creates a personal culture that is always striving to drive the fight.

Your "bandit" in this case, may be another human being, but often, it will be yourself — your habits and the daily activities and situations you get in as you go through life.

Crafting your *CATSHOT 13* plan is crafting your offensive attitude. We described the 13 steps necessary to develop your plan in Chapter 5.

These steps will help you craft a simple-to-understand and straightforward plan to execute. Your plan will work in the real world. It is not just theory. However, there will always be bandits lurking that will try to get you off your game, force you to react, and attempt to make you fail. Let's discuss how to thwart those negative forces.

Your Personal Learning Curve

The first thing to recognize is that by following your *CATSHOT 13* plan, you will take off like a catapult shot off of an aircraft carrier. Your performance will initially accelerate quickly. But, once you get airborne, you will lose some of that extra energy you got from the steam catapult.

You will find that instead of continuing to climb, your performance may plateau, or you may actually regress. It happens to Blue Angels in winter training and to major league baseball players, golfers, and other athletes in their off-season. Even the best experience performance regression at some point.

The difference between champions and the rest of the world is that the champs get out of their slump much quicker. They recognize it, make corrections, and start climbing the ladder of success sooner than the average person.

Navy pilot landing grades provide a great example. Individual Navy fighter pilots keep landing statistics for each time they come aboard an aircraft carrier. They have lifetime stats just like baseball players. These statistics are used to identify unsafe trends in pilot performance so they can be corrected quickly. This ensures the safety of the pilot, his aircraft, and the flight deck crew on the ship.

Just like with batting statistics, the pilots who consistently win the competitions are those who can recover from a landing slump the quickest. They have the confidence that they can do well because they have done well in the past. They have learned over time the things that can make their performance drop, and they quickly make the corrections necessary to fix the problem. Usually, on the next pass, they will find themselves right back at the top.

In contrast, those pilots who have lost their self-confidence, or who have not methodically analyzed their own performance, often take numerous passes to get back into form. In each case, the pilots and their aircraft were equally capable. The best aviators just better understood the human aspects of learning, and had visualized the best way to maintain peak performance. They were excellent at being their own coach.

During your CATSHOT 13 program, you will have your own bad landings now and then. The key to staying on your accelerated flight path to success is to first recognize it, then to have fun with it. Have fun analyzing yourself and figuring out how to improve.

You will find that most of the time, you do not have to rely on others to tell you what you are doing wrong. You will actually have more fun doing this for yourself and making your own corrections.

What You Can Expect the Bandit to Do

The *CATSHOT 13* program is designed for the real world. Because of this, you will learn to anticipate other humans and/or life situations that might throw you off your game plan and make you react. You will be shown tools, and you will develop some of your own, that will get you back to driving the fight as quickly as possible.

Here is a sampling of internal and external "bandits" that your *CATSHOT 13* plan can prepare you to address:

1. Your Health

- Mental capacity: Anything that prevents you from thinking clearly such as drugs and alcohol or lack of sleep

- Physical capacity: Anything that prevents you from being at your peak physical condition, such as poor nutrition or inconsistent or incorrect exercise

- Spiritual capacity: Anything that diminishes your motivation, such as naysayers, people with negative personalities, fear (fear of failure, fear of what others think about you or your plan), or other peer pressures

2. Your Resources

- Poor time management and prioritization, lack of direction, inability to make a decision, procrastination

- Poor use, or misuse, of your support and advisory system, such as friends, family, and your personal advisors and coaches

- Failure to properly budget for the expenses necessary to achieve your goals

3. Taking for granted or failing to recognize and therefore develop the natural skill sets and attributes you were born with

4. Failure to be honest about the state of one's own capabilities and, therefore, failure to put an effort into correcting deficiencies

5. Failure to work on developing a personality with a positive, optimistic outlook on life

When you lead with a positive approach to expanding your personal frontier of human achievement, you will take a positive approach to driving the fight and eliminating the possibility of these negative influences.

Ben Franklin's 13 Virtues . . . A Starting Point for Your SOP

You will develop your own list of positive attributes that you will want to embrace in *CATSHOT 13*. To get you started, here is a list that Ben Franklin developed over 250 years ago. He knew, even back then, that it was important to focus on the positive.

When you stay positive and drive the fight, you will naturally be defending against the negative.

Benjamin Franklin's 13 Virtues

Note: The one-word description and the quoted texts are Ben Franklin's words.
The author's interpretation follows.

1. Temperance: "Eat not to dullness; drink not to elevation." — Eat and drink nutritiously with correct proportions. Keep a clear, sharp mind!

2. Silence: "Speak not but what might benefit others or yourself; avoid trifling conversation." — Speak in positive terms, especially about others. Avoid gossip.

3. Order: "Let all things have their places; let each part of your business have its time." — Keep both your personal and business administrative activities organized.

4. Resolution: "Resolve to perform what you ought; perform without fail what you resolve." — Develop a good plan and execute what you plan.

5. Frugality: "Make no expense but to do good to others or yourself, i.e., waste nothing." — Be mindful of your money and use your resources to the positive benefit of yourself and others.

6. Industry: "Lose no time; be always [employed] in something useful; cut off all unnecessary actions." —

Be deliberate. Be efficient.

7. Sincerity: "Use no hurtful deceit; think innocently and justly, and, if you speak, speak accordingly."—Give others the benefit of the doubt; always be a gentleman or lady.

8. Justice: "Wrong none by doing injuries, or omitting the benefits that are your duty."—Don't abuse your position of authority, and don't unjustly gain personally at someone else's expense.

9. Moderation: "Avoid [extremes]; forebear resenting injuries so much as you think they deserve."—An eye for an eye, but don't overdo it. Make the punishment fit the crime.

10. Cleanliness: "Tolerate no uncleanliness in body, [clothes,] or habitation."—Look sharp personally. Keep everything ship shape. My personal saying is "Clean jets fly better." Cleanliness is a mindset that permeates individuals as well as organizations to make them more efficient.

11. Tranquility: "Be not disturbed at trifles, or at accidents common or unavoidable."—Take life's small hiccups in stride—stay positive!

12. Chastity: "Rarely use venery but for health or offspring, never to dullness, weakness, or the injury of your own or another's peace or reputation"—Focus your physical drives in a positive manner.*

13. Humility: "Imitate Jesus and Socrates." — Be humble, be positive.

*Note: We will substitute the word *Drive* for *Chastity* in this book to more accurately reflect the intent and meaning for the *CATSHOT 13* program, which is to focus your sexual/physical energy in a positive way.

Your SOP

In your *CATSHOT 13* plan, you will take these 13 virtues as a starting point and develop them into your own SOPs. You should always try to maintain a positive attitude no matter what challenges are thrown your direction.

As you boldly but deliberately take on challenges that stretch your current capability, you may experience outcomes that seem to others to be failures. They are only failures if you do not learn from them and take positive, corrective, and more intelligent action the next time.

Emergency Procedures — Boldface

Fighter pilots perform extreme maneuvers in extreme and hostile environments. Over time, they have developed a culture of anticipating for emergencies, and have prepared immediate action steps based on learning from the mistakes of those before them.

These maneuvers are written in the "immediate action procedures" section of the aircraft's operating manual and are in boldface print. They are therefore referred to as "boldface procedures."

Because you are about to subject yourself to an extreme environment in order to expand your personal frontier of achievement, you will need to develop your own boldface items as well.

Personal Crisis Planning—Being Prepared for the Unexpected

In addition to your positive, proactive approach to life's challenges and your goal to create opportunities out of failures, you must always be ready for the unexpected.

Not every situation has a boldface procedure to counter it, because sometimes a combination of events can create brand new problems that no one has yet encountered. You cannot plan for such situations specifically. However, you can do what the military does and create your own, personal crisis action plan. It will be designed to ensure you get the best information in the timeliest fashion, so that you can make smart decisions in response to whatever it is you will face.

Using Your Head

Every Navy aircraft operating manual has the same important warning written in it. This warning states that the SOP, Boldface Procedures, and Operating Limitations listed in the handbook are no substitute for good judgment.

In other words, the warning is telling aviators that there may be situations, which can develop, that are not addressed in the manual or where the "book" answer may not apply. Often, this is proven true even in legacy aircraft that have been operating for more than 30 years. Even with all the lessons learned and revisions to the manual made during the lifetime of that aircraft, not every situation can be anticipated or reasonably covered.

Using good judgment is truly the essence of becoming a Naval Aviator. A Naval Aviator critically thinks and questions, as opposed to a pilot who is simply performing rote skills.

Similarly in life, we want to help you become a "life aviator," not just a pilot! That is where *CATSHOT 13* will take you.

Points to Remember

- Learn the mental skills to "drive the fight," and do not focus on just having the proper equipment. You must also have the skills to use the equipment.

- Discuss the things that you know are going to happen, and add contingency planning for as many scenarios as you can imagine.

- Have a positive attitude about everything you do, and stay away from those who do not support you and believe in your dream.

- Consider all of the aspects of success that you can control — physical, mental, and spiritual health; economic and physical resources — and work to improve them.

POH Exercise

While most of the POH exercises included in this book have been fairly short, the following information is more of a description and explanation of the actual *CATSHOT 13* Daily Planning, Briefing, and Debriefing sheet that can be found online. You can follow along with the sheet that is included in your POH download or you can customize the information in your own logbook to suit your specific needs. Once your initial Effects-Based Life Planning is completed, you will spend most of your time using this "sheet." Each day you use it, you will refine and reinforce your Noble Calling, your interim goals, your *CATSHOT 13* goals, and then your top three goals for the current week. Your goals for the day should be traceable all the way back to your Noble Calling.

This process should be exhilarating and motivate you to achieve at your peak potential every day. It is a planner, a daily briefing and debriefing tool, and it can act as your personal logbook or journal.

Helpful Hint: The *CATSHOT 13* program is about creating a personal culture to win. With it, you will expand your frontier of achievement by creating great habits and improving on your health, as well as your personal and professional skills. The process is repetitive intentionally. Just like a Blue Angel, a TOPGUN pilot, or a professional athlete, you will learn to create the muscle and brain memory to progressively achieve at higher and higher levels. Below is a typical example and an explanation of what you will find in the *CATSHOT 13* POH:

CATSHOT 13 Daily Planner

Daily Briefing and Debriefing Sheet

Step 1. Fill in the date, day, and week of your *CATSHOT 13* program. Add your location.

Date: (____/____/_____)

Day ____ Week ____ of 13 [For example, Day 1 Week 1 of 13]

Your Location: _____

Step 2. Write down your Noble Calling, which you developed in the Effects-Based Life Planning exercise. Then take a moment to visualize yourself achieving this life goal.

Helpful Hint: After you begin the *CATSHOT 13* program for the first time, you will refine your Noble Calling almost every day until you begin to see a pattern develop. At some point, it will become rock solid—this is your goal, as it will become your guide in focusing all your energies and will CATSHOT you to success.

Passion

I am fired up today to pursue my Noble Calling, which is:

_____

_____

Step 3. Write down the top three interim goals you determined from your Effects-Based Life Planning that will be the most logical in helping you achieve your Noble Calling. Visualize yourself achieving these goals.

The Interim Goals (1 to 3 years) I will achieve in pursuit of my Noble Calling are:

1. _____

2. _____

3. _____

Step 4. Write down the top three goals you set for yourself for the current 13-week period of the *CATSHOT 13* program. Visualize your success.

My *CATSHOT 13* Goals for this 13-week period are:

1. _____

2. _____

3. _____

Step 5. Write down the top three goals that you plan on accomplishing this week. Visualize yourself achieving these goals.

Helpful Hint: You should be able to draw a logical thread from your Noble Calling through your interim and *CATSHOT 13* goals to these weekly goals. You will adjust these goals every week, based on your building-block approach and self-coaching techniques. When your plan is working well, you will increase the difficulty level or achievement level each week until you achieve your *CATSHOT 13* goals.

The Top Goals for this week that will help me achieve my *CATSHOT 13* goals are:

1. _____

2. _____

3. _____

Step 6. Write down what you are doing this day to help maintain your ability to exercise your free will.

Helpful Hint: See Chapter 2 for the discussion on free will for ideas. Additionally, the POH contains recommended emergency action boldface procedures you can use against life's bandits that will continually try to get you off track from your goals.

Free Will

I am maintaining/using my free will today by:

_____

_____

Step 7. Now write down your specific goal for the day.

Helpful Hint: This goal will most likely be in an area that you determined needed improvement from the previous few days. It also may be specific to your success with an important event like a job interview, presentation, or athletic competition. No matter what, if you accomplish one goal today, this should be it.

Today's Focus

My Specific Goal for Today is: _____

_____

In the POH, there will be a space for you to debrief this event. You can use the goods or others format or indicate achievement with a YES or NO response. (See Chapter 6 for "goods and others" scoring.)

Step 8. You will then start your To Do (or achievement) list for the day. This list will be broken down into several personal performance-related categories such as health, professional skills, and life skills. You will then write down the administrative To Do list you need to achieve that day.

Helpful Hint: In the *CATSHOT 13* program, we recommend you always work to improve your health and your professional and personal skills as part of your daily routine. These need to be part of your culture. Therefore, you will see them listed in the POH as daily requirements.

Health Achievements for the day:

1. Physical training for the day is . . . [List what your physical training plan is for the day.]

    Physical training debrief . . . [In the POH there will be a space for you to debrief how it went.]

2. Mental training for the day is . . . [List what mental activities you are doing that will train and stimulate mental alertness.]

    Mental training debrief . . . [In the POH, there will be a space for you to debrief how it went.]

3. Spiritual energy training for the day is . . . [List the things you will do throughout the day to boost your spiritual energy and keep you performing at your peak. These can include listening to motivational music, meditating, or taking a walk outdoors.]

    Spiritual energy training debrief . . . [The POH has a space for this to be debriefed.]

Skills Achievements for the day:

List one or two professional skills you are working on refining throughout the day. This can be something very specific, such as public speaking, communicating, or writing, and it should be aimed at improving your overall performance. These skills should also complement your weekly and *CATSHOT 13* goals.

Debrief your performance . . . [Fill in how it went using a goods and others format.]

Life Skills (Ben Franklin's Virtues)

These are skills that you should always be working on in the background. Some may even become your specific goal for the day. For example, if you are trying to lose weight and have been having trouble with portion control, temperance may be listed as your specific goal for the day. Otherwise, even if it is not a specific goal, it will still be a goal, along with the other virtues (life skills), that you work on throughout your day. These virtues should be debriefed every day in a goods and others format. See the list of Ben Franklin's 13 Virtues and their definitions in Chapter 7 of this book, as well as in the *CATSHOT 13* POH.

1. Temperance: GOOD or OTHER

2. Silence: GOOD or OTHER

3. Order: GOOD or OTHER

4. Resolution: GOOD or OTHER

5. Frugality: GOOD or OTHER

6. Industry: GOOD or OTHER

7. Sincerity: GOOD or OTHER

8. Justice: GOOD or OTHER

9. Moderation: GOOD or OTHER

10. Cleanliness: GOOD or OTHER

11. Tranquility: GOOD or OTHER

12. Drive: GOOD or OTHER

13. Humility: GOOD or OTHER

List your day's To Do list, including some professional and some personal tasks as needed.

Today's additional administrative To Do list:
Did I complete these tasks? (Y/N)

- _____

- _____

- _____

- _____

Step 9. Fill in your schedule for the day. There will be room in the POH for you to debrief how it went.

Helpful Hint: Make sure you allow extra time for the real-world interruptions to your schedule that will most likely occur. Additionally, set aside time for maintaining your spiritual energy by taking a break when you need it; this will help you perform better in the long run. A common mistake for those who are striving to be more successful is trying to do too much in one day. Remember, slower is often faster.

On the next page, you will see a simple example of what your day's schedule might look like.

Day's Schedule

<u>Planned Activities</u>   Did I Execute?

(Fill in planned activities)   (Indicate YES or NO)

5:00 AM: _____

5:30 AM: _____

6:00 AM: _____

6:30 AM: _____

7:00 AM: _____

7:30 AM: _____

8:00 AM: _____

8:30 AM: _____

9:00 AM: _____

9:30 AM: _____

10:00 AM: _____

10:30 AM: _____

11:00 AM: _____

11:30 AM: _____

12:00 PM: _____

12:30 PM: _____

1:00 PM: _____

1:30 PM: _____

2:00 PM: _____

2:30 PM: _____

3:00 PM: _____

3:30 PM: _____

4:00 PM: _____

4:30 PM: _____

5:00 PM: _____

5:30 PM: _____

6:00 PM: _____

6:30 PM: _____

7:00 PM: _____

7:30 PM: _____

8:00 PM: _____

8:30 PM: _____

9:00 PM: _____

9:30 PM: _____

10:00 PM to 5:00 AM: _____

Step 10. Throughout the day, take notes on how you think you did. For those areas that do not have a built-in debrief format, write down what you learned here. Pay specific attention to noting what you feel that you can do better. Visualize yourself doing it better.

Today's general debrief — lessons learned and things to do better tomorrow:

- _____

- _____

- _____

- _____

Step 11. Write down at least one thing you were grateful for today. This is a common practice for many people who are attempting to put their life in perspective.

Today, I am grateful for (one or more things): _____

_____

_____

Step 12. Think very deliberately and select one goal that you would like to achieve tomorrow. To determine what that goal should be, review your day and look for trends or one big goal that seems to be eluding you. Put as much effort into accomplishing that goal as needed to achieve it for tomorrow.

Tomorrow my specific goal will be (one goal): _____

_____

_____

Step 13. Celebrate your achievements for the day. End the day on a positive note. Visualize yourself successfully achieving your goals tomorrow.

For the latest version of the actual two-page *CATSHOT 13* Daily Briefing and Debriefing Sheet, please go to http://catshotgroup.com/productsservices/books.

Chapter 8:

Earn Your Wings—Go Beyond Piloting and Become a Life Aviator

Beyond Your Wings

There were a dozen of us, all in dress blues with covers (military term for hat or cap) square and our backs straight. We were standing at attention in the training wing of the Navy Commodore's office.

The Commodore and the Chief of Naval Air Training (CNATRA), a one-star Admiral, stepped up to each of us, one-by-one, and pinned on our Wings of Gold. It was official. After hundreds of hours in the air performing grueling exercises in the T-28 Trojan, T2 Buckeye, and the A4 Skyhawk, we had qualified to become Naval Aviators. We had arrived!

Or so I thought.

The Admiral turned to us and said, "Congratulations! You have earned the opportunity to continue learning."

From that moment on, the learning never ended. Our Wings of Gold were only the beginning. We all left the training squadron and went on to the various types of jets we were assigned to fly. I was fortunate, as I had been selected to the newest jet in the inventory, the F/A-18 Hornet.

Seasoned veterans trained my classmates and me. Many of the vets had been on hundreds of combat missions in Vietnam. It was in their powerful shadows that I learned the true meaning of being a Naval Aviator. They all had many important things in common, not one of which had to do simply with flying.

- They were all so good at what they did that they made extremely difficult tasks look easy.

- They always seemed to be able to make the right decision, quickly and decisively, even when they didn't always have all the information.

- They each questioned everything, never believing the first report they read or heard.

- They used their intuition, their sixth sense, a lot, both in sizing up people and in sizing up the enemy in combat.

- They always kept perfection in their hearts, even when they knew they would never achieve it.

- They were persistent. Once a decision was made, they went for it. They made it work.

- They were survivors, both in the air and on the ground. They could work their way to a target area full of bandits and make it back time and time again.

- They never lost situation awareness—ever.

- They each had strong character, impeccable ethics, and a love of their country.

That is when I knew what it meant to be a Naval Aviator, not just a pilot. I was not just performing a task, I was upholding a noble tradition of excellence.

Years later, with numerous overseas deployments, multiple tours at TOPGUN, and after commanding an F/A-18 Strike Fighter Squadron, a Carrier Air Wing, and the Blue Angels, I like to think that I embodied those same characteristics.

Even later in my career when I was much more senior, I had the opportunity to work at the highest levels of the military directly for three- and four-star Admirals and Generals—they still had the same mindset.

Their experience, cognitive ability, personalities, and use of both synthetic and actual creative imagination were incredible. They never seemed to run out of energy as they traveled around the globe. They effortlessly stayed hyper-focused for incredibly long hours every day. They also did it for very little pay.

Talk about a Noble Calling — the American people are very lucky! These men and women are great examples of the Performance Triad at work.

Living with Passion

What sets these individuals apart, and what you are striving for with your *CATSHOT 13*, is a personal culture of excellence. You can achieve this through repeated training, until the *CATSHOT 13* battle rhythm becomes second nature. Just like those four-star Admirals and Generals.

You will make your chosen path look easy to those around you, even though it is not. On this path, you will always be striving to do everything better in every part of your life, whether it be personal, business, or a chosen hobby. You must have perfection in your heart, and when you do, you will be a Life Aviator, not just a pilot.

Points to Remember

- Elite performers create a lifestyle of constant improvement and relentless innovation. You will not reach this level in 13 weeks, but you will come just a little bit closer to the person you want to be.

- Elite performers, or Life Aviators, strive to be better in all aspects of their lives, not just one. They understand that they must reflect their Noble Calling in their daily routines.

- Elite performers are always learning, always questioning, always growing. This constant desire to improve gives them the confidence to use their judgment when "the manual" does not apply. They always have a "personal crisis plan."

- Elite performers are not afraid to move out of their comfort zone to find new answers and better ways to do things.

POH Exercise

Learn to push yourself to the next level with this exercise:

- List your goals and their associated *CATSHOT 13* tasks you have selected—then ask, are they at the right level?

- Find three different colors of highlighters.

- With Color #1, mark through the tasks that you have done before and know will be fairly easy to accomplish.

- With Color #2, mark through the tasks that you have not done before, but are sure you can figure out or accomplish if you really push yourself.

- With Color #3, mark through those tasks that you have never even attempted before and/or that you have no idea how you will accomplish just yet.

What color are most of your entries?

Do you have some of each color?

Having some of each color will help you build momentum by allowing you to first accomplish some of the easier tasks so you can quickly move on to those tasks that are new to you but you are confident you can do. You will also need to have at least a few tasks that are a little scary and unfamiliar, so you can really see what you are capable of.

Too many easy tasks, and you are not pushing yourself to achieve at a new level. Too many scary and unfamiliar tasks, and you may find yourself discouraged or out of energy pretty quickly.

As you progress with your *CATSHOT 13* program, you are going to get better and better at what you have chosen to accomplish. To continue making progress, you need to understand what is going to happen to you, how other people may view you, and how you will begin to view yourself.

Section 3:

Expand Your Frontier of Achievement

Your Winning Legacy!

Imagine climbing vertically through the clouds after your successful CATSHOT from the 1,092-foot deck of a Nimitz class aircraft carrier. You feel the freedom that only comes with flight. You skillfully complete dozens of maneuvers behind the controls of your F/A-18 fighter jet, just like you practiced on the ground in your "chair flying" exercises. Your instructor threw crisis after crisis at you, and you came out on the other side, unscathed.

Now you safely land back aboard the USS George Washington where your crew is waiting. You shut down your Hornet, climb out, and make your way through the incredibly noisy flight deck, ducking the hot and dangerous jet engine blasts coming from the other aircraft.

That mission is over. It was a roaring success.

Congratulations, you achieved your goals, step-by-step.

Your efforts to align your personal Performance Triad paid off.

Now what? Relax, retire? No way! You have only just begun. The journey toward your Noble Calling is a life-long trek.

Each mission, each CATSHOT, is only an interim step toward your greater goal — your Noble Calling. Now that you have tasted success, you have greater responsibility.

First, you have a responsibility to yourself.

You have to continue to work toward winning on your next mission. Even though the last CATSHOT and flight were awesome, you have to prepare for, and execute, your next CATSHOT. Next time, you will fly even better than the last time.

Second, you have a responsibility to those around you, to your "wingmen."

You never know when your achievement and mastery will spark the passion in the person next to you, or unleash their free will, or motivate them to focus. You now have a responsibility to be a motivational force in their lives by living your Noble Calling. If you stop being true to yourself, those around you will notice, even if they cannot describe what they see.

Very quickly, you will sense that you have a new aura around you — an aura of success, an aura of achievement.

It is a powerful force that comes with living true to your passion.

Your winning legacy will be based not on just one achievement, but on a lifetime of achievements. You must never stop growing, so make the *CATSHOT 13* process part of your personal culture. Evolve it; adapt it over time as you improve.

Success via *CATSHOT 13* is not about any single achievement or any one goal you have reached. It is about developing a long-term mindset that refocuses you from the goal immediately in front of you to creating a lifetime legacy.

Let's take a look at the future!

Chapter 9:

Your Personal Mystique—The Mindset and Aura of a Winner

John Wayne in the Break, Slim Pickens in the Groove

"**Y**ou are only as good as your last pass!" my Landing Signals Officer (LSO) yelled as I landed with a less-than-stellar performance.

It was my first combat air patrol on this particular overseas combat deployment, but it was my second tour of duty as a Fleet Squadron F/A-18 Pilot. I had made hundreds of "OK" passes before today. But none of that mattered, because I had become a leader, a person that others looked to for guidance.

Regardless of whether you have one landing under your belt or more than a thousand, landing a high-performance jet aircraft on an aircraft carrier is difficult—especially at night when the weather is bad and the deck is pitching back and forth. Each attempt to land is called a "pass," and pilots are routinely graded on each one they make.

One of the most dramatic maneuvers required to land on an aircraft carrier is the "combat break."

Jets returning from combat air patrols try to get back to the ship as quickly as possible. This reduces the time the carrier has to navigate a straight line. Straight lines are not good when there is an enemy around, as it gives them time to get you in their sites.

The standard procedure to minimize time is for returning jets to fly over the ship at 350 knots (more than 400 mph) at 800 feet, parallel to the ship and in the same direction the ship is traveling.

While directly overhead, the aviator rolls left, pulls back on the stick and holds 4Gs as he or she makes a 180-degree turn for a "break," which bleeds off airspeed. Once slowed, the pilot will lower the landing gear and flaps. He continues a left descending turn until he arrives on the extended centerline of the landing area about a quarter mile behind the ship. This location is referred to as the groove. He then rolls wings level and flies his aircraft straight to touchdown.

If done right, the pilot will be "on and on" all the way to touchdown, which means he flies the correct glide slope and line up parameters and will catch the number three of the four wires strung across the flight deck. When he catches a wire, it is called an arrestment, or a "trap."

Because there are no airspeed limits over water as there are over land, returning pilots will often return much faster to the ship in order to reduce the time to recover. It is considered a rite of passage to be able to execute that same maneuver just described, but much faster.

Typically, you will see the break maneuver executed at more than 600 miles per hour. At that speed, a skilled pilot will be able to get the landing gear and flaps down just in time to land aboard the ship, if he does it *just* right. Pulling off a perfect landing in this fashion is associated with the coolness under pressure similar to the characters in a "John Wayne" movie, and considered very impressive.

For a young pilot, there is always the question in his mind as to when he is ready for such an aggressive move.

Every once and a while, you come across a young buck who has had one or two successful breaks leading to several successful passes at the lower speed. He thinks he is now ready for the big time. He misjudges his capabilities, attempts the aggressive maneuver, and fails to properly reach the parameters for the landing.

Being out of parameters, and a threat to himself and those on the flight deck, the Landing Signal Officer will wave him off. Now, instead of saving time and looking like a hero, he is wasting time and flying in shame.

When this happens, it is said that "He was John Wayne in the break, but Slim Pickens in the groove," in reference to the sidekick who was not as cool.

* * *

The moral of the story is: As you progress through life and move through your *CATSHOT 13* program, you will have hits and misses, and people will judge you based on your "last pass." Just remember that when you balance your personal Performance Triad and head toward your Noble Calling, you will become more consistent with every pass. You will expand your ability to achieve.

Regardless of whether you are a student, an athlete, a businessperson, or a grandparent, you will be creating or adding to your legacy of achievement with every pass. As you build on your body of work, you will naturally develop an aura and mystique that you may not have ever experienced before.

People will begin to look to you for direction and approval. They also will begin to expect more from you. You will find that even you will begin to expect more from yourself.

This new-found attention may tempt you to become over-confident and try your own John Wayne move.

Be careful! We rarely talk in negative terms in the *CATSHOT 13* program; however, this is one time we will tell you: Don't be John Wayne in the break and Slim Pickens in the groove. Remember, you are only as good as your last pass. You do not want to have to rebuild your reputation all over again because you misjudged your capabilities.

Instead, build yourself up in a methodical way. *CATSHOT 13* will help you develop the skills to do that. You will be ready for your own 600+ mph break sooner than you think.

Don't Believe the Press Clippings

"That was awesome!"

"You guys were perfect! I've never seen anything like it!"

"You were flawless! You made that look so easy!"

As Flight Leader of the Blue Angels, I was inundated almost every day with comments like these. Almost every day, a reporter would write a news article, or a fan would tell me in person how great my teammates and I were.

We *were* good, but we were far from perfect.

Fortunately, we had a culture of briefing and debriefing that constantly reminded us that we always had room for improvement. We were not perfect. And we certainly were not invincible.

Although the shows look incredible and simple from the crowd's perspective, I can tell you that from the first practice to the very last show, we were dead serious about what we were doing. We never took anything for granted.

We spent long hours debriefing each mission and relentlessly picked away at the smallest details. That was the mindset that kept us from believing we were perfect. It kept us safe to the very end of the season. That is the winning spirit that you want to have.

In the airshow business, the community of aviators continually polices its members. The brash and reckless are not welcome.

Regardless of your occupation, it is important to take compliments with a grain of salt. Thank those who compliment you, and appreciate that they enjoyed working with you. However, always know in the back of your mind that you can always improve.

Never think you are so good, the rules no longer apply.

You *can* fly too high and too fast.

While our *CATSHOT 13* program encourages you to push your overall limits in the form of goals and dreams, we also ask that you list your operating limits and create SOPs. This process helps you focus on those boundaries you are able to push, while being mindful of those boundaries that you must respect.

As you progress through the *CATSHOT 13* program in subsequent rounds, you may find that your operating limits expand and that you can change some SOPs. However, you should make these alterations to your limits and goals in a methodical way with a lot of thought.

Recklessly moving forward is one of the worst possible examples you can set for others. I have friends who are no longer with us because they forgot this important step in the process — enough said.

Understand the addiction of pushing the envelope — and *CATSHOT 13* professionalism.

Why would a person push the envelope beyond established norms?

Often it is a simple case of peer pressure. You get talked into going beyond your limits and your SOPs at the urging of others.

This is easily done when you do not have established operating limits and SOPs that you can see and understand clearly. It is easy to move beyond your limits if you haven't thought about where those limits might be or why you should have them.

The second reason is a deeper, more insidious phenomenon — often more dangerous. It comes from within you. In effect, you can find yourself becoming addicted to pushing your boundaries.

For example, as part of your *CATSHOT 13* program, you decide you are going to expand your performance and achievement capability, right up to the established limitations. These limitations have been deliberately set either by you or your professional community. It is important you understand *why* those limits were established.

At first, you are learning. Progress comes at a steady pace. You have some plateaus and valleys, but in general, you keep improving, little by little. This pattern continues right up to the moment that you hit your limit.

Each time you performed better. You expanded your limits. You gained a new sense of accomplishment. Now all of a sudden, you are at the end.

Your professional limits, or the deliberate, well-thought-out limits you set for yourself, prevent you from going further. Your sense of achievement is stifled. You have a gap in your spiritual health. You find you are addicted to the process, and you want to continue. What do you do?

Simple, find another goal or area that needs improvement and put your heart into trying to perfect that goal. In other words, work to reach the limits of *all* of your goals, instead of focusing on the one goal you have reached, even if you are positive you can take it to the next level. Wait until you have the time to review that goal, when your adrenaline rush is over.

If you artificially set your limits too low or you think your professional occupation's governing body has it wrong, then make a deliberate, methodical appeal to yourself or to your organization. Work internally or with your group to think through the reasons for the limitation, and change it, if that is the right course of action.

It is important to recognize and understand your addiction to improvement. It is a good thing if you use that energy in a positive way. Limits are put in place for a reason, usually having to do with safety for either yourself or others that could be affected by your actions.

CATSHOT 13 is all about pushing you to the next level of achievement. However, we encourage goal setting and identifying limits to allow you to improve incrementally and safely.

Congratulations, on your successes! Just remember that you have a responsibility now to yourself and to others to be even better! Use your *healthy* addiction to improvement as new fuel for your passion to reach your Noble Calling.

Points to Remember

- Strive for Perfection in Your Heart
    - Understand that you can be excellent, but never perfect.
    - Always be a student of your art form.
    - Continue to learn and be open to new ideas.
    - Never stop being a relentless innovator.

- Establish Credibility in Your Noble Calling

    - Learn to admit when you are wrong. *CATSHOT 13* will test your ability to be honest with yourself. If you are not, you will not improve as quickly as you can.

    - Take a positive approach to your 13 Virtues, your SOPs, and your operating limitations.

    - When you make a mistake, take ownership and responsibility for your actions.

    - Learn from your mistakes and do it better next time.

- Winning and *CATSHOT 13*

    - Like a fighter pilot who survives the mission and wins, your mission to improve is not over. You still have to come back aboard the ship and land safely.

    - Be sure to debrief and prepare to put your best effort in being ready to do it all again tomorrow.

- You can and should feel proud of your accomplishments. However, remain humble and realize that as good as you are, you can always improve.

- Revisit your Noble Calling and develop another set of goals that are beyond those you just accomplished and that will bring you even closer to your Noble Calling.

- Be honest with yourself about your motivations to achieve. Take the time to mediate and realign with your Noble Calling, working hard to avoid taking risks due to an addiction to the adrenaline of breaking barriers.

POH Exercise

Write down how you believe you will feel when you realized that you have accomplished your *CATSHOT 13* goals.

- Was it harder or easier to accomplish than you anticipated when you started?

- What are you most proud of accomplishing?

- How did your family and friends react to your achievements? How did that make you feel?

- What do you realize you could have done better, if your passion, free will, or focus was stronger?

- Have you achieved your Noble Calling? If not, realize that as great as you are, you can be better and begin the *CATSHOT 13* process again. If so, it is time to aim even higher with your Noble Calling. Restart your *CATSHOT 13* process with your new ultimate passion.

- What lessons or advice do you have for those who look up to you and want to emulate your new-found success?

Chapter 10:

Keeping Your Winning Momentum—Your Next *CATSHOT 13*

"**B**oss is OK," I call out.

" . . . Jack is OK . . . ," says the pilot 1,000 feet behind me on landing rollout.

On down the line go the radio calls as all six of us let those behind and in front of us know that we are at a slow, safe taxi speed after we touched down. Just moments before, we were flying past the crowd at 400 knots and 150 feet above the ground in a very tight Delta Formation.

My wingman and I have completed the final maneuver of the first show of the new season. After we taxi back in front of the crowd that has come to watch, we dismount and walk to the show line to greet our audience.

For the past three months, we have been in winter training where we isolated ourselves to focus on perfecting our demonstration. Although we had plenty of real-world distractions during training, we now have the added challenges of traveling to different show sites every week.

Starting this day, we would perform in front of thousands of spectators at each show for the next nine months. We would have a different battle rhythm that would include all of the distractions of travel. We would also dedicate much of our time to visiting schools and hospitals, and talking with the local media.

Recruiting and public outreach, not flying, would be our primary mission on the road.

This first landing of the first show of the season marked a new beginning. A fresh, new effort would be built on the successes of the last three months. Keeping our momentum as a team, as well as our individual momentum, was critical to our mission—not to mention, critical to everyone's safety.

It was time to evaluate and dedicate ourselves to our next *CATSHOT 13* cycle.

Just like Blue Angels after their winter training effort, you must keep your momentum going forward with your next cycle of goal-setting and improving your personal performance.

Renewed Dedication to *CATSHOT 13* and Your Noble Calling

After you complete your first 13-week *CATSHOT 13* cycle, I know you will see that you have made headway toward the intermediate goals of your Noble Calling. For those of you still struggling to find your Noble Calling, this first cycle will bring you a little closer to identifying and understanding what really drives you to succeed.

It is a rare person who achieves all of his or her goals in one *CATSHOT 13* round. If you are one of those people, then you are probably aiming too low!

For most of you, your first and future *CATSHOT 13* cycles will be tough, yet rewarding. You will hit many of your goals, and miss a few. You may start out strong and then lose momentum, sometimes through loss of energy, sometimes due to unforeseen challenges that seem insurmountable. This is all to be expected.

Every time an athlete moves to a higher level or a business leader rises through the ranks, the competition to win and move forward becomes tougher. A new level of dedication must be applied with every step up the ladder.

When doctors complete their residency, engineers change jobs, or entrepreneurs decide to sell their business, the change can drain his or her energy. It is a challenge to keep up your momentum as you make the necessary changes in your life.

During these periods, it is imperative that you rededicate yourself to *CATSHOT 13*. These steps can help you strengthen your personal Performance Triad and move forward with purpose.

At the end of each 13-week CATSHOT cycle, you will begin the process again. With your experience of a *CATSHOT 13* in the rearview mirror, everything should be more refined in future rounds.

As you work on your new direction in life, you will need to refine your Noble Calling and identify what facts and assumptions may have changed. It is the perfect time to renew and refresh. Use your experience to your advantage.

Much as I did at the Blue Angels and many times since then, I enjoy this process of review and renewal. It prevents life from getting static. It really is the thrill of the journey that many successful people talk about. So have fun with it.

The lessons learned in your first *CATSHOT 13* cycle will help drive your future cycles. Here are some key points to keep in mind as you progress through future *CATSHOT 13* rounds:

- **Keep what works.** If your planning was done well, your overall yearly goals will align with your Noble Calling. Many of the professional and personal skills, as well as your gains in physical, spiritual, and emotional health, should be congruent with this next phase in your plan — your next *CATSHOT 13*. Keep doing what worked well in the past.

- **Reassess your goals and parameters for your new reality.** Really dedicate time to reviewing the facts and assumptions you used during your first *CATSHOT 13* round. They may now be different. You must account for those in your new plan.

- **Stay humble and be patient with your slow and steady progress.** Don't be overzealous now that you have expanded your frontier of achievement. Too much overreach and impatience can set you back. On the other hand, make sure you are challenged. Make sure your next steps are a logical progression from the ones before.

I keep each *CATSHOT 13* cycle fresh by looking at the 13-week cycles as seasons. If you go from one season directly into the next, you will complete four cycles every year. That is 4X more than most people do in a year!

My cycles all include physical training. I never focus only on business goals, but always add physical, mental, and emotional health goals. For example, I do not have a goal of running a 5k in one *CATSHOT 13* cycle and 10k in the next cycle, and so on. Instead, I like to vary my physical training programs for the seasons, setting goals in the various types of activities I will be doing during those seasons. For me, the big ones are alpine skiing in the winter, aerobatic flying and motorcycle riding spring through the fall, and boating, water sports, hiking, and biking in the summer.

I also like to align my business activities in a similar fashion. I look at each new quarter with renewed interest and very focused goals — they are always aligned with my Noble Calling.

Just like winter training at the Blue Angels, I look forward to each new season and new activities.

To keep my focus, I followed Ben Franklin's lead. He carried a sheet of his 13 virtues with him throughout his lifetime in an effort to continually improve. I carry a list of some of my personal SOPs and operating limitations. This helps keep me focused and dedicated to my personal improvement. I highly recommend you do the same.

When in doubt, remember the simplicity of the Performance Triad.

Despite the successes you will have, you will likely face the threat of straying away from the principles that got you here.

Increased success often leads to more demands on your time. This equates to loss of liberty and your ability to exercise your free will.

The more successful you are, the more demands and duties will be placed on you. Maintaining focus will be a challenge.

No matter how much passion you have for your original goals, losing these two critical elements of the Performance Triad can derail your progress.

Protect yourself with your well–thought-out operating limitations, boldface procedures, and SOPs. If you are in a leadership position, look for ways to offset some of these challenges to your free will and focus by having the right employees and teammates relieve the burden.

But in all cases and at all times, you must keep your eye on the ball. Remember the big picture! Why are you doing all this anyway?

The key is your Noble Calling.

Points to Remember

- One *CATSHOT 13* will not define your success. It will be a continuous string of them throughout your lifetime that will define the lasting value of your winning culture. Throughout all of this, your big Noble Calling should remain the one touchstone that you can always rely on to keep you going.

- In aviation, which is very unforgiving, we learned to accept, write down, and adhere to limits. Developing your own operational limits and SOPs and remembering to incorporate Benjamin Franklin's 13 virtues (or your own virtues) into your daily life will bring you long-term success. You must develop the habits of a winner.

- When you begin to lose your energy or feel you are losing your way, focus on your Noble Calling and redefine all you do in terms of reaching your higher purpose.

POH Exercise

Pull out your Standard Operating Procedures and Operating Limits that you developed in Chapter 5. They were Steps 9 & 10 of your *CATSHOT 13* program.

Visualize yourself completing your current C-13 cycle. As discussed in Chapter 5, the time will come to revisit what you entered for Steps 9 and 10 in your first 13 weeks, and then ask yourself:

- Now that I have reached a new level of achievement in the pursuit of my goals, are these goals still relevant?

- Which SOPs do I need to re-write?

- Have my operating limits changed?

Now, write down how these answers will change your behavior in your next round of *CATSHOT 13*.

Chapter 11:

The Lasting Value of Your Personal Winning Culture

H ow do you measure achievement? Are you really targeting your Noble Calling? Are you thinking big enough?

These are the questions world-class performers ask themselves on a regular basis, throughout their entire lives. The elite never stop working to achieve more, to reach higher and higher goals.

As the leader of the Blue Angels, my teammates and I always tried to keep the real reason we were doing what we did in the back of our minds. The stated reason the team existed, of course, was for recruiting. We kept metrics to indicate that we did a very good job of that. We showcased Navy and Marine Corps pride and professionalism every week and the results were evident at the recruiting centers.

But, for each of us, our personal Noble Calling went well beyond recruitment numbers.

Every week after our Friday practice show, it was tradition for the team to meet with young men and women brought in by the Make-A-Wish Foundation®. They taught me a lesson I will never forget.

Friday practice shows were notoriously difficult as we were always trying to get comfortable and oriented to the new show site. Typically, on those days, the post-mission debriefs were long—we always found plenty to correct for the following day's live audience performance.

As a result, we often wanted to go straight to the "ready room" to discuss how we could improve, especially after a particularly stressful practice.

But even though our passion to perfect our performance was strong, we always took the time to meet with the Make-A-Wish kids.

Their genuine interest in us and in the practice demonstration that we had just performed was breathtaking. Their courage in the face of often-fatal illnesses was inspiring. The smiles on their faces were priceless.

To me, that was the bigger, unwritten mission, or Noble Calling, of the Blue Angels. We were there to inspire these kids and inspire the nation. Yet, as it turns out, they inspired us more.

Those kids always put my own ego into perspective for me. They did not care how tight our formations were or how low or fast we flew to the ground. They wanted to see Blue Jets fly by and to be proud of their military. Maybe they could get a glimpse into something they would likely never see again or get to do themselves. They wanted to meet and talk to a Blue Angel to see what it was like. They wanted to live the moments through us!

That experience taught me two things that have stayed with me.

First, in the airshow business, we had a responsibility to the crowd. Just as a business leader has a responsibility to his or her employees and shareholders. At each airshow, my goal was to inspire the crowd by showing how well my teammates and I could perform in the extreme environment of a low-altitude jet demonstration — while making them feel safe.

Second, it made me think of my Noble Calling in a different way. My number one Noble Calling will always be my family. That is a given. But when it comes to my professional efforts, the lessons I learned on the importance of giving back were much more powerful than I could have ever imagined.

I always felt extremely humbled after meeting so many great people at the crowd lines afterwards. These people put things in perspective for me and served to check my ego. Ever since that experience, I strive to achieve that same sense of purpose in everything I do every day.

I hope that the success you achieve with *CATSHOT 13* will be as rewarding for you as my own experiences have been for me. I also hope you find that your Noble Calling in some way includes giving back. Because often, the spark you give someone by demonstrating what you have done with your passion, will often come back to inspire you even more!

If you have not yet tried *CATSHOT 13*, I encourage you to challenge yourself and go for it!

For those of you who do take up this challenge, I urge you to begin today. Now that you have read through the book, begin your *CATSHOT 13*. Only you can make sure it delivers on its promises, because you are in charge of your life plan.

Make sure you:

- Identify your inspired **Noble Calling**, or your **Passion**

- Develop a plan for relentless innovation, or harnessing your **Free Will**

- Cultivate an unwavering persistence and concentration, or **Focus**

- Maximize achievement by creating your personal **Performance Triad**

Organize the building blocks necessary to take you to the next level and achieve your goals in a safe, methodical way. Embrace challenge and opportunity responsibly, and be sure to give back to your team, your family, and your community.

CATSHOT 13 will give you the mindset of a winner by incorporating continuous improvements in your daily life. You will learn how to stay motivated over time and how to use your success to develop a winning legacy that impacts your family and your community well into the future.

Points to Remember

- Creating a legacy for the future is what following your Noble Calling is all about. Short-term goals merely keep you focused and give you the steps to walk toward your "true north" or your Noble Calling.

- Look beyond yourself to find fulfillment. True wealth comes from providing service to others and inspiring them to find and follow their passion.

- Shortcuts to success do not exist, because success is not a destination, but a way of traveling through life. *CATSHOT 13* is a map for creating that travel plan.

POH Exercise

Visualize yourself completing your current C-13 cycle and celebrating your achievements. Then visualize yourself taking that energy and passion and applying it to your next

CATSHOT 13 cycle. Finally, visualize yourself ultimately achieving your Noble Calling! You are on your way!

A Final Note

Quotes like the following are what I hear from many of my fellow TOPGUN instructors and Blue Angel teammates, even years after we had moved on to other professions.

"Grateful for being part of such a noble profession!"

"A privilege and honor to have been given the opportunity to focus on pushing the limits of human achievement every day... and doing it for such of noble cause, protecting the freedom of our nation."

Few get the chance to be brought into the fold of such elite organizations where the culture is organized around an incredible alignment of passion, free will, and focus! TOPGUN and Blue Angels definitely have it, and so do the individuals who are part, or ever were part, of those teams.

We are all grateful because we were given the chance to contribute to a vision that was greater than ourselves. We made a difference in people's lives and to our nation.

We were also grateful because we each learned how normal people, given the opportunity to form their own Performance Triad, could push the limits of human achievement into frontiers they had previously thought unattainable.

That experience made an indelible imprint on each of us as we pursued other careers, each striving to duplicate that same tremendous sense of fulfillment we attained by having a higher purpose. The list of their individual achievements and what each has done for their communities and families is eye-watering.

CATSHOT 13 is my way of passing on what I learned. It does not matter if you are a grandmother setting great examples for her grandchildren, a business leader, or a student. If you dedicate yourself to a purpose, using all of your passion, free will, and focus, you will be able to push out into new frontiers you never thought possible.

Believe in yourself and your dreams. Give yourself credit for every small victory. Stay positive in the face of every adversity and never give up! You will achieve something greater than yourself!

# # #

About the Author

Expanding the frontier of human achievement, and doing so wherever performance matters. This has been a lifetime focus for Rob "Ice" Ffield from the beginning.

He excelled in many sports from an early age, and was exceptionally accomplished in alpine ski racing and soccer. Leading as team captain in both disciplines, he accumulated numerous personal and team wins at state and regional competitions through to his college years.

His focus on innovation and the pursuit of perfection reached world-class levels during his unprecedented string of naval career milestones, which included two tours as an air-combat instructor at the prestigious Navy Fighter Weapons School, TOPGUN; selection to lead the world-famous Blue Angels; and combat tours while in command of a strike fighter squadron and carrier air wing. His infectious enthusiasm for "making things better" and his aggressive operationally oriented leadership style were the catalysts for numerous individual and team awards and his rapid rise through the naval ranks.

Knowing teamwork and personal excellence principles could be applied to anyone, regardless of accomplishment level, type of profession, or stage in life, Rob was inspired to share them in his first book, *Building a Culture to Win: Expanding the Frontier of Human Achievement*. There, Rob laid out the framework for building elite teams, much like the ones on which he served.

His newest book, *Building a Personal Culture to Win: Expanding Your Personal Frontier of Human Achievement*, expands on the same proven concepts to demonstrate effective ways of developing the habits and honing the necessary skills required to become a top performer, individually. The *CATSHOT 13*™ process is the first step.

This uniquely crafted 13-step, 13-week program is Rob's personal system for excellence. Just like top corporate leaders, entrepreneurs, athletes, artists, and fighter pilots, those looking to push themselves to the world-class level can be taught how to perfect the art of becoming their own coach, aligning their life goals with a Noble Calling, and living with guided passion every day.

In the private sector, Rob Ffield is a dynamic, inspirational leader known for building successful strategies. By founding CATSHOT Group, LLC, Rob has encouraged businesses and individuals to perform at their maximum potential by providing strategic planning services, seminars and elite team training to those who want to use proven practices to accelerate their ability to achieve the most challenging goals. He is an innovator and a well-respected consultant to some of the world's most elite and recognized organizations. He also is passionate about individual success and has continually provided transformative solutions to assist others in their quest to expand their personal frontier of human achievement.

Index

O

P

Notes

Notes

Notes

Notes